Monarch's
DICTIONARY OF INVESTMENT TERMS

Edith Lynn Beer

Published by MONARCH PRESS
A Simon & Schuster Division of Gulf & Western Corporation
Simon & Schuster Building
1230 Avenue of the Americas
New York, New York 10020

MONARCH PRESS and colophon are trademarks of Simon & Schuster, registered in the U.S. Patent and Trademark Office.
Designed by Irving Perkins Associates
Manufactured in the United States of America
10 9 8 7 6 5 4 3 2 1

Library of Congress Catalog Card Number: 82-61052
ISBN 0-671-45497-8

ACKNOWLEDGMENTS

My thanks go to the many experts in the financial world who were willing to help me in my research. Among those who took time from their busy schedule to share their expertise were: Richard Blodgett, Kenneth M. Fox, Donald Gross, Donald Fox, Peter C. Osborne, Jacques Luben, Sheridan Nofer, Neil T. Eigen, and E. B. Storms. My thanks also go to my editor, Valerie Levy, who seems to smile through all adversity.

Very special thanks go to Professor Garland C. Owens, Ph.D., professor of accounting at the Graduate School of Business, Columbia University, a Certified Public Accountant, and business consultant. Professor Owens was the first one with whom I discussed the idea that a book explaining investment terms in simple language was needed. He immediately encouraged the project and declared his readiness to help.

I am grateful to the Brooklyn Business Library as well as to the library of the American Institute of Certified Public Accountants. My thanks also go to Chemical Bank, United States Trust Company of New York, Irving Trust, Merrill Lynch, Pierce Fenner and Smith, Inc., and Dean Witter Reynolds, New York Stock Exchange, the American Stock Exchange, and The New York Futures Exchange.

EDITH LYNN BEER

CONTENTS

PREFACE

I was waiting in my bank to see one of the vice presidents when I heard the following conversation between the banker and a young couple who were obviously considering buying a house or condominium.

Banker: "The best mortgage for you might be an *adjustable rate mortgage*. Of course, there would be *points* involved."

The young man: "I think I may know what *adjustable rate* is, but could you explain exactly what is entailed?"

The young woman: "Could you also explain *points*? I was hoping for some simple, straight mortgage."

Banker: "A straight mortgage? I wouldn't recommend it. With the economic situation as it is, a whole new approach has been taken."

The young woman: "I hate to interrupt, but is there a list of all the different types of mortages that do exist?"

Banker: "There are lists but I am afraid they do not include the latest ideas in mortgages."

And there I thought is a real need—a list of financial terms that investors could have at their fingertips not only before they take out a mortgage, but also before they invest in bonds, stocks, the money instrument market or anything else in the world of finance. Suppose this young couple had had a list and explanation of every type of mortgage and all the terms related to borrowing at their fingertips—how much better could they cope and express their particular needs when talking to the banker. They also would know what alternatives are available if this banker does not offer them what they want.

Most financial dictionaries cover either only one subject or cover every aspect of investing from A to Z. If you are planning to invest in a bond, and would like to feel more comfortable with the terminology, you might not know under what letter to look. "B" for bond won't tell the whole story. If you are not quite sure under which chapter heading to look for a particular term, the index at the back of the book will guide you.

Monarch's Dictionary Of Investment Terms covers each financial subject—such as stocks, money instruments or loans—in separate chapters. Each chapter is in turn in alphabetical order so that you can not only find a term within a subject quickly but also get a feel of all terms needed to express yourself well on that particular subject. This book is intended only to expose and define financial language and *not* to advise the reader how to invest.

Our recent and continual economic fluctuations have given birth to many new financial terms. Other terms are not as new, but seem to be because we are using them more due to present financial and economic situations.

Whether new, rarely used or often used, these terms have all been gathered in this book and defined in clear and simple terms.

While this book does not intend to give advice on how to invest, it is hoped that it will make the ins and outs of the financial world and its jargon more meaningful.

BONDS –

AAA or **Aaa:** the highest-quality rating a bond can receive. The ratings are given by several independent rating services, two of which are *Moody's* and *Standard & Poor's. Standard & Poor's* ratings range from AAA, AA+, AA, AA−, A, A+, A−, BBB, BB, etc., to C. *Moody* expresses its ratings Aaa, Aa1, Aa2, Aa3, A1, A2, A3, A, Baa, Ba, Caa, Ca and C.

Bonds issued for and by different types of businesses cannot be compared. For example, there is a difference between an AAA rail bond and an AAA utility bond.

accretion: a bond's rise in principal value to full face value at maturity. This rise occurs when a bond is purchased below face value. (See *deep discounted bond* and *discounted bond.*)

accrued interest: interest earned but not yet due and payable. For example, if a bond paying interest on January 1 and July 1 is bought on February 3, the buyer will receive on July 1 an interest payment for one half year. Since the seller owned the bond for 34 days of that 6-month period, the seller will receive the interest accrued during those 34 days from the buyer.

amortization: the process of the gradual extinguishment of the premium money above par on the books of the issuer and the holder of bonds. Discount bonds are accreted to par while premium bonds are amortized to par. In amortization the buyer's yield and capital gain are less. The issuer has a gain.

basis point: 1/100 of 1 percent yield. 50 basis points would mean ½ percent higher yield.

basis price: price expressed in terms of yield to maturity; annual rate of return. A case in point is a 5-year bond whose yield is 10 percent. During the bond's lifetime the country's prime rate goes down to 9 percent. Obviously, the bond's 10 percent yield would become valuable and increase the bond's price. The bond's yield as compared to other bonds' yields would be expressed in basis points.

bearer bond: bond whose principal and interest are payable to whoever has physical possession. The bond is not registered in anyone's name.

bond: an interest-bearing certificate of debt usually issued by a government or corporation which obligates the issuer to pay the principal amount back at a specified time.

bond anticipation notes (BANS): notes issued by states and municipalities to procure interim financing for projects that will be eventually funded by long-term issues.

bond calendar: a schedule of newly issued bonds which will be available to the public shortly.

bond options: the right to buy (call) or sell (put) within a designated time on specified treasury bills, notes and bonds. The cost of money (interest rates) during the remaining life of the bond will determine the price. (See *stock options.*)

callable bond: bond whose issuer has the right to redeem the bond before the maturity date by paying some specified call price. The right of the issuer to redeem the bond before maturity is cited on the face of the bond certificate.

convertible bond: bond which at the option of the holder may be converted into other securities of the corporation. When bonds are convertible into stocks, the stocks into which they are convertible must be authorized at the time the bonds are issued.

The owner of the convertible bond will find it profitable to exercise his or her option if the value of the stock into which it is being converted should subsequently exceed the value of the bond at the conversion price. The price of the bond usually relates to the price of the securities into which it is convertible.

Convertible bonds are attractive because they allow the purchaser the safety of a bond or an increase in value through the conversion option.

The corporation gains whenever a conversion to securities takes place because the fixed charges of the corporate debt are reduced.

corporate bond equivalent also know as **equivalent bond yield:** the annual yield on non-interest-bearing bonds (also bills, notes and short-term papers) adjusted to be comparable to the yield quoted on coupon-bearing obligations.

The principle of equivalent yield also exists in our personal lives. If a friend came up to you and said, "Lend me $1,000 at 10 percent for 1 year and on the 365th day of the year I will pay you back not $1,000 but $1100," you might answer, "I have that $1,000 in a 10 percent savings account which pays interest semiannually, and it is automatically reinvested so that I get compounded interest. Roughly speaking, in 6 months I'll get $50 interest, and by the end of the year the $50 will have earned me another $2.50. Therefore, $1,000 invested at 10 percent compounded earns me $102.50 and not $100 interest."

Your friend might then reply, "Whatever you lend me I will give you an 'equivalent yield' except that I will pay you the sum at the end of the year."

coupon: a series of separate due notes attached to a bond, each to be detached at its maturity date for the purpose of collecting interest.

credit risk: the chances of loss because the issuer of a bond is not able to pay back completely or in part the principal and/or interest. (See *AAA*.)

current coupon: coupons of those bonds issued in the past whose yield is more or less the same as the yield being offered on newly-issued bonds. For example, Debbie Smith bought a bond two years ago which gave her a 10 percent yield. New bonds are yielding approximately 1/8 of 1 percent more. Debbie considers the bond she owns to be within the line of the current coupon offerings.

current issues: most recently offered bonds and notes.

current yield: the annual return of an investment.

cushion bond: a bond which has a high coupon and which is callable below the current premium price. Such bonds sell at a lower premium than comparable noncallable bonds because of its callability below the current premium price. Cushion bonds, because of their high coupon, are popular among investors in a downside market.

debenture bond: an unsecured bond backed only by the credit standing of the issuer rather than by specific property or mortgage. Government bonds are usually unsecured since generally their only backing is taxes. (See also *revenue bond* and *special assessment bond*.)

deep discount bond: a bond which is considerably below maturity price, giving the investor an opportunity for a long-term gain. For example, several years ago John Colt bought a $1,000 bond paying 6 percent interest and due in 10 years. John Colt had no way of knowing when he locked his money into a 6 percent yield that interest rates would go sky-high. His accountant is now suggesting that he sell his bond because he could use the loss on his income tax. John Colt's $1,000 bond is now selling on the bond market for $842. The new buyer will continue to receive $60 annually or 6 percent of one thousand dollars. But because the new buyer bought the bond for only $842 he is actually receiving 10 percent on his investment. Even though he only paid $842 for the bond, he will receive the full $1,000 at maturity.

default: failure to fulfill a contract such as interest or principal due at the designated time.

discount bond: bond sold at a price lower than its face value. Carol bought a 5-year bond at $1,000. After 2 years she decided that she needed her money sooner than she had anticipated. At the time Carol wanted to sell the bond, it sold for $995 on the open market. Carol decided to take the $5 loss of the discounted bond. At maturity the bond will pay the full face value.

disintermediation: the act of large transference of funds from financial institutions such as savings in savings banks and other time deposits into stocks and bonds because the return on stocks and bonds is higher. Time deposits are no longer attractive.

dollar bond: the face value of the bond exclusive of the interest it pays or the amount the coupons yield. The advantage of dollar pricing is that it is easy to compare the prices of the various issues. The coupon yield has to be figured separately.

effective yield: the yield of the principal (gain or loss) plus the interest of a bond bought at above or below par calculated at maturity when there is a capital gain or loss as well as interest income.

Eurobond: a bond issued in Europe and developed with the Eurodollar. The bond may be in the particular country's currency or in dollars. Eurobonds are often issued by the United States for the benefit of its overseas operations. They are bearer bonds and paid without withholding tax deductions.

extension swap: prolonging a bond's maturity through swapping for a similar one with a longer current maturity. The swap may also be accomplished by selling a bond just before its due date, when it may tend to be slightly above par, and buying a similar bond with a longer maturity date.

face value: the amount the company issuing the bond promises to pay at maturity.

Fannie Mae: a nickname for Federal National Mortgage Association, a government-sponsored corporation created to buy old mortgages. Not guaranteed by the government.

Federal Home Loan Mortgage Association also known as **Freddie Mac** and **motorcycles:** Similar to *modified pass-thru mortgages*. These bonds are government-guaranteed.

fixed-dollar security: nonnegotiable instrument such as bank deposits and government savings bonds that can be redeemed at a fixed price at some predetermined fixed schedule.

flat trades also known as **flat income bond:** a bond in default and therefore without accrued interest. Some corporate revenue which are not in default and also trade without interest.

floating-rate bond: bond whose yield is adjusted every 6 months to bring the bond into line with the current market rate.

flower bond: old, low-coupon government bond selling at substantial discount and acceptable at par price in payment of federal estate taxes when owned by the decedent at the time of death.

general obligation bond: municipal security whose credit rating is determined by its taxing powers, past credit rating and reputation.

gilt-edged bond: highly-rated bond (see *AAA*) whose issuer has a long reputation for paying interest without interruption.

Ginnie Mae: a nickname for Government National Mortgage Association. Similar to *modified pass-thru mortgage securities*; these are guaranteed by the government.

give up swap: the loss that occurs when a block of bonds is swapped for another block offering lower coupon yields. This may be done to incur a loss needed for taxes.

Glass-Steagall Act: a law passed by Congress in 1933 which prohibited commercial banks to own, underwrite or deal in corporate stocks and corporate bonds.

governments: another term for negotiable U.S. Treasury securities.

guaranteed bond: bond whose interest and/or principal

is guaranteed by a company other than the issuer. Usually found in the railroad industry when larger industries or allied companies want to make the bond more attractive to the buyer. Some investors consider these bonds risky as the guarantee does not necessarily appear on the face of the bond but may be in a separate agreement.

income bond: bond which repays the principal but only pays interest when earned. Sometimes the accumulated unpaid interest may be claimed against the corporation when the bond becomes due. Generally these bonds are not high-grade investments.

indenture of a bond: the written agreement under which bonds are issued. An indenture contains the maturity date, interest rate and other terms. The term comes from an obsolete custom of placing the copies of an agreement together and tearing an irregular edge on one side. Matching of the edges of any two documents at a later date was considered proof of the identity of the documents containing the agreements.

interest: the percentage a borrower pays a lender, usually paid semi-annually. In the case of a bond, interest may be paid by coupon. (See *coupon.*)

junk bond: bond in default, or bond considered high-risk because of low rating.

long bond: bond whose maturity is many years off.

long coupon: a bond which may have more than one coupon, but which has one coupon in particular (usually the first coupon) which has a longer period to its due date than others or than is standard. (See *short coupon.*)

market value: the present trade value of a bond. The amount the present market allows for a bond.

marketability: the readiness with which one can trade a bond. It is a good market when the secondary market is active.

maturity: the date a bond, note or other indebtedness becomes due and payable.

modified pass-thru mortgage securities: bonds conceived by the government to help those banks holding low-interest-rate mortgages. The concept acts like a bond in that it has a coupon and maturity with a variable amount paid out each month. This amount is a combination of interest earned on the invested amount and whatever principal was paid off (pass-thru) on the underlying mortgages.

mortgage bond: property, equipment or other real assets pledged as security. If a corporation is forced to default in the payment of its bonds, secured obligations possess priority to the extent of the value of the property pledged. Not to be confused with a general mortgage bond, which may be outranked by one or more other mortgages.

municipal notes (MUNI): short-term notes issued by municipalities in anticipation of funds from bond issues, receipts or other proceeds.

odd lot: a term used in the bond market when less than one trading unit or less than even units are purchased. (See *round lot*.)

OID: (original issue discount): newly issued bond sold as if it were a discount bond. (See *discount bond*.)

par: the face value of a security at maturity or the amount at which a debt security contracts to pay out at maturity. Often signifies the dollar value upon which interest will be paid.

par bond: a bond selling at face value.

paydown: term describing situation when the par value of maturing securities exceeds those presently being sold on the market; also refers to the government market and the refinancing of the national debt.

pay-up: 1) any borrower's willingness to pay a higher rate in order to get funds; 2) the loss of cash incurred by swapping into higher-priced bonds.

pick-up: the term for a higher yield when bonds are swapped for another block of bonds offering higher coupons.

point: a term used to quote the change in the price of a bond. One point represents $10 or a percentage of $1,000, so that a bond which rises 3 points gains 3 percent of $1,000 or $30 in value. An advance from 95 to 98 would mean in dollars from $950 to $980 for each $1,000 bond.

premium: 1) the difference between the face value and the actual higher price at which an issue is trading; 2) the amount paid in excess of the face value in order to call a bond before maturity.

premium bond: a bond selling above par.

prepayment: a payment made ahead of the scheduled payment date.

presold issue: a bond issue which is sold out before it reaches the market.

principal: the face amount of a bond; commonly known as par value.

RANs: abbr. of Revenue Anticipation Notes. Issued by states and cities to finance current expenses in anticipation of income from nontax sources. For example, a municipal stadium may be financed by RANs with the thought that the stadium's income will pay off the notes.

rating: worthiness of a bond. (See *AAA*.)

red herring: a preliminary prospectus filed with the SEC before securities may be issued. The prospectus is marked with red ink: "Not a solicitation, for information only."

refunding: a new issue of bonds to replace existing bonds. (See *paydown*.)

registered bonds: bond whose owner is registered with the issuer; the name of the owner also appears on the face of the bond, and the proceeds are payable only to the owner.

registered coupon bond: same as a registered bond except that the attached coupons are payable to any bearer.

regular way settlement: terms describing normal procedure of bond purchased whereby they are usually delivered on the day following the transactions. Other securities such as stocks take longer.

reinvestment rate: 1) the rate at which an investor can reinvest interest payments received from coupons or other securities; 2) the rate at which proceeds from a sale or maturity of a bond can be reinvested in the present market.

relative value: comparison of one bond to another in terms of relative maturity, interest, yield, risk, liquidity and return.

reopen an issue: the decision of the U.S. Treasury to sell additional notes rather than issue new ones.

revenue bond: a municipal bond backed by revenues from rents, charges or tolls.

round lot also known as **full lot:** term for trading units; over-the-counter bonds trade in units of 100; on the exchanges in units of 1.

seasoned issue: a well-liked bond because it has a good resale value and sold well when originally issued.

S.E.C.: abbr. of Securities and Exchange Commission. An arm of the federal government created to protect the investor against malpractice and misinformation in the securities market. All new bond and stock issues must be registered with the S.E.C., which enforces disclosure rules on all new security issues and supervises the activities of all investment companies and counselors in the United States.

secondary market: the market where bonds and other securities are *re*sold.

sector: bonds similar in type, maturity, rating and/or coupons.

serial bonds: bonds issued at the same time but that mature serially (staggered dates) and usually with interest rates varying for the different maturity dates.

series bonds: groups of bonds usually issued at different times and with different maturities (Series A, Series B). These bonds are under the authority of the same indenture.

shopping: when selling or seeking a bond, attempting to obtain the best price by calling several dealers.

short bond: bond having a short current maturity.

short coupons: coupons or interest due to the bond owner very shortly; a coupon payment period below the usual 180 days. (See *long coupon.*)

sinking fund: the sum set aside out of the company's earnings to pay off an issue of bonds. The company will either purchase or call the bonds according to the terms of the indenture. Part of the written agreement under which bonds are issued may require a sinking fund.

special assessment bond: bond backed by the power of the government to assess particular individuals for benefits presumably received in the form of public improvements financed by the bond issue.

take out: 1) to sell a block of bonds or securities and buy another block at a lower price, thus generating funds. For example, if John Smith decided to sell his bond at $1,100 and buy a new one at $1,000 par, his takeout would be $100; 2) to take the owner of the securities completely out of the market. This term is used by bond brokers or security brokers.

tax & revenue anticipation notes (TRANs): similar to TANs, except the source of revenue may be taxes and other revenues such as federal aid.

tax anticipation notes (TANs): notes issued by the government to provide funds for expenditures until taxes or other revenues can pay off the notes.

term bond: an issue of bonds which all mature at the same time.

Tigrs, Lion or Cats: certificates denoting that one owns the bond or the coupon of a particular U.S. Treasury bond which is held by a trustee. In essence, one owns either the zero coupon bond or the coupons stripped from the bonds.

treasury bill or note also known as **T-bill:** a non-interest-bearing discount security issued by the U.S. Treasury to finance the National Debt. The income in discount bills is in the increase between the purchase price, which is discounted, and the full maturity value. If, for instance, the Treasury decides to offer issues of $1,000 notes discounted at 10 percent, the purchaser would only pay $900 (10 percent of $1,000 equals $100; $1,000 less $100 equals $900) and receive $1,000 at maturity. Treasury bills are fully taxable. The minimum round lot is $10,000.

U.S. Dollar Bonds: a term used in the Eurobond market to state the cost in dollars of bonds being sold in the Euromarket denominated in U.S. dollars.

U.S. Savings Bonds: term that usually refers to a series of bonds issued by the federal government. Some series are discount type; The income from these bonds is taxable. Sometimes the government refers to these series by letters such as "E" and "H."

visible supply: those bond issues scheduled within the next 30 days. (See *bond calendar.*)

when issued trades (WI): term referring to the period when a bond is announced and sold but has not yet been issued; the bond is traded "when, as, and if issued."

yankee bond: a foreign bond issued in the United States, registered with the S.E.C. and payable in dollars, usually the debt of a foreign sovereignty.

yield curve: a graph showing, as of a predetermined date, the different yields to maturity on bonds similar in every respect except their maturity.

yield to maturity: the calculation of a bond's annual return from the principal, plus annual interest, at a fixed future date. The calculation is rather complicated; bond yield tables are available.

zeros: a discounted bond issued without a coupon.

STOCK – MARKET TRADING TERMS

arbitrage: the purchase of foreign exchange, stocks, bonds, silver, gold, or other commodities in one market for sale in another market. For example, one can purchase gold on the London market and sell it on the Paris market; similarly, exchanges of securities may also take place in a merger.

auction market: another term for the various stock exchange markets where buyers compete with each other and sellers compete with each other for the most advantageous price.

authoritarian: term describing an investing approach whereby the investor makes the selection of stocks by following the lead of assumed experts.

averages: term used for the various, rather elaborate formulas to measure stock trends. The formulas include stock splits and stock dividends, which are not to be confused with *dollar cost averaging*. (See *Dow Jones Averages*.)

balance sheet: a company's annual financial statement including the assets, debts, liabilities, available capital and stockholders' interest in the company.

bear: one who thinks the market will decline.

bear market: a term signifying a decline in the market.

bid and **asked:** the *bid* is the price offered at any time for a security or commodity, and the *ask* is the price requested. The quote, also known as the quotation, is the bid and asking on a security or commodity. For instance, a quote on a given stock may be 20.25 bid and 20.50 asked. In other words, the highest price a buyer wanted to pay was $20.25, and the lowest the seller was willing to take was $20.50.

Big Board: term for the New York Stock Exchange.

block: a large amount of stock in round numbers, popularly considered to be 10,000 or more.

blue chip: a stock that is low-risk because the company has a reputation for reliability, quality and the ability to make money and pay dividends.

blue sky laws: laws enacted by various states to protect the public against security frauds. The expression supposedly originated with a judge who ruled that a particular stock held as much value as a patch of blue sky.

board room: the room in a club or broker's office where leading stock prices are displayed electronically or on a ticker tape. Before the days of electricity, the prices were posted on a board.

book: a ledger in which the specialist in a stock records the exact buy and sell orders as the receipts from the stockbrokers are received. (See *specialist*.)

book value: an accounting term used to denote a company's assets.

broker: an agent who has passed a test to determine his basic knowledge in securities, who is registered with the S.E.C., and who may charge a fee to buy and sell securities, commodities, and other properties for the public.

bull: one who believes the market will rise.

bull market: the term used to express a rise in the market.

call: the right to buy a fixed amount of stock at a specified price within a given time.

callable stock: preferred stock that may be redeemed by the issuing corporation.

capital stock: all stocks in a business including common and preferred.

cash sale: a cash transaction on the floor of the stock exchange which calls for delivery of the securities the same day. Deliveries usually take 5 days.

certificates: the paper denoting ownership of a security. The certificates use watermarked paper and delicate etchings to make forgery difficult. Unless the certificate is registered with a company or broker, loss of a certificate may be irredeemable.

churning: a method to generate brokerage commissions; an unethical and in some cases illegal practice of trading and turning over a customer's securities faster than necessary, purportedly for the customer's good.

commission: the fee charged to the public for purchasing or selling securities or commodities. The agent who carries out the public orders is known as a *commission broker*.

common stock: securities which represent an ownership interest in a company allowing certain voting rights. Management considers the stockholder when dividend payments, stock dividends, stock splits, recapitalizations, mergers, expansion, sale of new securities and use of rights are normally planned. Common stockholders assume a greater risk because their claims are junior to bondholders and other creditors of the company. The preferred stockholder is limited to a fixed dividend and in case of liquidation of assets has prior claim on dividends. However, the common stockholder may reap greater profits in the form of capital appreciation, dividends and extra declared dividends.

competitive trader also known as **registered trader:** a member of the exchange who trades in stocks on the floor for an account in which he has an interest.

conglomerate: the result of mergers and takeovers of companies and corporations in complex deals involving cash and/or securities, and culminating in the production of diversified, nonrelated items and services. The parent company may cite savings in common facilities, personnel and general staff services. The diversification promises a larger economic base for the stockholders, participation in new growth areas and in some instances an avoidance of the cyclical effect of a single industry.

consolidated balance sheet: a balance sheet showing the financial condition of a corporation and its subsidiaries.

convertible preferred stock: stock that may be exchanged by the owner for common stock or another security, usually of the same company, as determined by the original issue.

covering: paying for a security previously sold short. (See *short selling.*)

cumulative preferred: refers to preferred stocks which provide that if one or more dividends are omitted, these omitted dividends must be paid before dividends are paid on common stocks.

cumulative voting: right of a shareholder to cast as many votes as the amount of shares the shareholder owns. The shareholder may cast these votes for each director, or the accumulated amount for one director, or divide among any number of them. For instance, Mary Smith owns 1,000 shares in XYZ Company. She is sent a list of ten nominees to the board of directors. She may cast 100 votes for each director or 1,000 votes cumulatively. She may decide to give her vote of 1,000 to one director or divide her voting rights into 300, 300, 300 and 100 thus voting for only four persons.

day order: an order to buy or sell to last only for the day it was placed. If it is not executed by the end of the day, the order is canceled.

dealer: agent who buys over-the-counter stocks for his own account and sells to a customer from his inventory. Any security may be bought or sold by any securities firm which cares to do so. The bulk of such business is done in securities that are not actively traded on the stock exchanges. Dealers belong to the National Association of Securities Dealers, Inc., an association of brokers and dealers in the over-the-counter securities business. NASD has the power to expel members who have been found to be unethical.

debit balance: in a margin account, the portion of stocks unpaid and owed to the broker.

depository trust company: the central securities certificate depository where security deliveries are done by computerized bookkeeping, often avoiding the physical movement of stock certificates.

directors: those who supervise the managers of a corporation, bank or other business institution. Federal and state laws prescribe as to who may and may not be elected director to certain types of business institutions. For example, New York State Business Corporation Law (sec. 701) states that each member of the board of directors shall be at least 21 years of age. Federal and state laws in general define a director's rights, duties, restrictions and responsibilities. Directors are elected by shareholders and decide, among other matters, if and when dividends shall be paid.

discretionary account: account set up by the customer that allows the broker in part or fully to decide the purchases or sales of securities or commodities, including selection, timing, amount, and price to be paid or received.

diversification: spreading one's investments among different companies in different fields.

dividend: the amount of payment decided by the board of directors to be made to the shareholder for each share held. Preferred shareholders generally receive a fixed amount which was determined when the preferred share was issued.

dollar cost averaging: taking a fixed dollar amount at regular intervals and buying stocks whether they are up or down; a means of building up equity in the stock market.

Dow Jones Industrial Average: a stock market average reached by a rather complicated formula. The average is calculated on the basis of 30 major industrial corporations whose total closing prices are divided by a number which compensates for past stock splits and stock dividends.

Dow Jones Transportation Average: average made up of the 18 major transportation companies including airlines, railroads, trucking firms and a freight forwarder. (See *Dow Jones Industrial Average* for description of how the average is obtained.)

Dow Jones Utilities Average: average of 15 major utilities geographically divided. (See *Dow Jones Industrial Average* for description of how the average is obtained.)

Dow theory: a famous system developed by the editors of the *Wall Street Journal* which calculates the trend of the market (up or down) by taking the industrial and rail averages (see *Dow Jones Industrial Average*) as a barometer of the market's future. Some believe the Dow Theory predicts the business cycles or longer states of recession, depression or prosperity. Some issues will rise and fall with the waves of the cycle, but other issues may have special conditions which will not make them part of the wave. For example, the market might be bearish but if there is a heavy need of gold and people are investing heavily in gold, gold mine stocks might be up.

equity: in stocks, the term is synonymous with the liquidation value of the company.

exchange acquisition: a way to buy a large block of stock on the floor of the Exchange; the broker can solicit the various sell orders and ask to have them lumped together and matched with a large buy order. The price to the buyer may be net or on a commission.

exchange distribution: a way for a broker to sell a large block of stock by lumping together many small orders for the same stock. The commission is built into the price.

ex-dividend: means without dividend; because of the scheduling of the dividend, dividends are declared quarterly; as of a given date, sellers keep the most recent dividend.

ex-rights: means without rights. A corporation may issue more stock to raise money, and offer the right to its stockowners to buy additional stock at a discount from the prevailing market price. There are a given number of rights per share that the stockholder may sell, thereby owning the stock without rights.

extra: extra dividend issued in the form of stock or cash.

floor: the trading area on the New York Stock Exchange.

floor broker: a member of the stock exchange who can buy or sell any listed security on the floor and who may execute orders for his or her firm.

formula investing: investing according to one of many theories on economic waves, cycles and other techniques. (See *fundamentalist*, *authoritarian*, *diversification*, and *technical analysis*.)

fundamentalist: an approach to investing in which the

selection of stocks is based on value, quality and yield or growth.

good delivery: delivery of an unencumbered security complying with the contract of sale and transfer title to the purchaser.

good 'till canceled order also known as **GTC** or **open door:** an order placed by a broker to buy or sell at a specific price that remains open until executed or withdrawn.

growth stock: a stock of a company whose earnings are at a faster growth rate than the Gross National Product. (See *gross national product.*)

guaranteed stock: term that usually refers to preferred stock.

hedging: an effort to stabilize the value of a stock by selling or buying for future delivery.

inactive stock: a stock having a low volume of trade.

in and out: a purchase and sale of a security within a short time of each other. The trader is usually interested in a quick profit.

independent broker: broker who has a seat on the stock exchange and will execute orders for those firms who do not have a seat or for those brokers who have more business than they can handle.

institutional investor: any large accumulation of capital for investment such as pensions or trusts of large organizations including universities, banks, insurance companies, etc.

investment banker: the middleman between the corporation issuing new securities and the public. The investment banker buys outright the new issue which is then sold to individuals and institutions. Thereafter the issue is traded in one of the securities markets.

investment company: firm that sells stocks and uses its capital to invest in other companies to achieve capital growth and capital gain. Investment companies sell two types of stocks: closed-end, which are salable on the open market, and open-end, which can only be sold back to the issuing investment company.

Investors Service Bureau: a service provided by the New York Stock Exchange answering all written inquiries concerning stock investments. The bureau's services include clarification of exchange operations, and advice on tracing allegedly fraudulent securities.

letter stock funds: unregistered stock purchased at 25–50 percent below market price; the shares are held until the company prospers so that the shares can be offered publicly at a profit.

leverage: ratio between common stock equity and debt. For example, equity of 10 percent and 90 percent debt would be highly leveraged.

limited price order: an order to either buy or sell securities only at a specified price.

liquidity: in the stock market, the ability of a security to withstand buying and selling at reasonable price changes.

load: the cost of commissions and distribution of mutual funds (open-end investment); the cost is incurred in purchases but usually not in sales.

long position: another way of expressing ownership of securities; "I am long 250 IBMs."

margin account: a type of account where a customer borrows money to pay for a certain percentage of the cost of securities. The margin is the money borrowed. The broker may use his or her credit to borrow the money from the bank for the customer's account; there is a charge for borrowing this money. The broker holds the securities for the customer as collateral. The Federal Reserve sets the maximum amount which may be borrowed. Margin requirements may be lowered to induce more trading or raised if the government fears overbuying or speculation fever.

Margin accounts are also used in commodity future trading. They are risky because if the stock goes down, the customer is required to add money to maintain the margin.

margin call: request to the customer to put up collateral in the form of securities or cash with the broker. The call is made when the borrowed amount exceeds the amount the government allows the client to borrow.

market order: an order to buy or sell securities at the best price available to the customer at the time the order is placed.

market price: the most recent price at which a security has been sold.

Member Corporation: a securities brokerage firm, organized as a corporation, with at least one member of the New York Stock Exchange as a director and a holder of voting stocks in the corporation. When the brokerage firm is organized as a partnership with at least one general partner who is a member of the New York Stock Exchange, Inc., the firm is known as a *Member Firm.*

merger: the taking over by a stronger company of a more passive company by direct acquisition of the other's assets. The dominant company usually continues under the same name. No conglomeration is created by a merger. (See *conglomerate.*)

Moody's Investor Service: a statistical service founded in 1903 by John Moody. Moody's merged with Dun and Bradstreet in 1961. Moody's services are used by private investors as well as banks, brokers, corporations, and every other conceivable financial institution. Moody publishes reports such as *Widely Held Common Stocks, Advisory Reports, Bond Record, Dividend Record, Bond Survey, Stock Survey, Transportation, Public Utilities, Over-the-Counter Industrials, Industrials, Banks and Finance, Municipals and Governments.*

NASD: abbr. of National Association of Security Dealers,

Inc. An organization for brokers and dealers in the over-the-counter securities business.

NASDAQ: abbr. of National Association of Securities Dealers Automated Quotations. An electronic system that provides brokers and dealers belonging to NASD with price quotations on securities traded over the counter.

net change: the price change of a security from one day's closing hour to the next day's closing hour.

new issue: a new security being put on the market by a corporation.

New York Stock Exchange Common Stock Index: a means of calculating composite price movements of all common stocks listed on the Big Board.

no-load fund: an investment company that does not make a sales charge for the purchase of its shares.

noncumulative: preferred stock whose unpaid dividends as a rule remain unpaid. The opposite of *cumulative preferred.*

odd lot: stocks traded in units of under 100.

off board: a term used for securities not executed on a national securities exchange but rather over the counter.

open-end fund: an investment company that continually issues shares as it receives new capital or that stands ready to redeem shares at net asset value.

option: the right to buy or sell at a specific price within a given time.

order good until a specified time: a limited price order which is to be canceled if not executed within a specified time. Jane Smith says she wants to buy 100 shares of XYZ stock provided the price goes down to 35 a share by the end of the week (Friday 4 P.M.); otherwise, the order is to be canceled. Ms. Smith has given an Order Good until a Specified Time.

overbought: term describing a security which may rise in price because of sudden intense buying; some may be of the opinion that such a security may be overvalued or overbought. The reverse situation, when people sell a particular issue in quantity, causing a good security to go down in price, is known as *oversold.*

over-the-counter: method of issuing securities for those companies which may not meet the requirements for trading on the Big Board or their regional exchanges. The dealers may or may not be members of a securities exchange, but must be members of the National Association of Security Dealers.

par: the face value assigned to the share by the company's corporate charter; does not determine the market value of the common stock. Par may often signify the dollar value upon which dividends on preferred stocks are computed.

participating preferred: preferred stock which receives regular dividends but is so chartered that once the common stock holders receive their dividends, the preferred stock holders receive extra dividends when possible.

passed dividend: omission of scheduled dividend.

penny stocks: stocks selling at less than 3 dollars a share. These are mostly over-the-counter stocks and may be speculative.

percentage order: an order to buy or sell a certain amount of a security only after a fixed number of shares have already been traded.

pink sheets: daily over-the-counter security quotes.

point: in stocks, 1 point represents $1. If a stock goes up 1½ points it gains $1.50. If a stock goes down 2 points it loses $2. Not to be confused with bond points. (See *point* in Index.)

preferred stock: stock promising prior claim on the company's earnings. Dividends are paid at a specified time before common stock shareholders receive theirs, and in case of liquidation, preferred stockholders have priority in all claims. Preferred stock may be *participating*, *cumulative*, or *convertible*.

premium: See Index.

price-earnings ratio: the formula whereby the cost of a stock is divided by its earnings for a 12-month period. XYZ common stock sells on the market for $30 and pays $2 dividend. The price-earnings ratio is 15 to 1.

primary distribution: the original sale of newly-issued securities.

prospectus: the circular disclosing important material about new securities which must be given to the investor to protect the investor. New securities must be registered with the Security Exchange Commission.

proxy: written authorization given by the shareholder that someone else may represent him or her and vote the shares.

proxy statement: pertinent information required by the S.E.C. for stockholders about the stock and their right to vote when solicited for their proxies.

Prudent Man Rule: a law in some states that a trustee may invest only in securities which will preserve the capital and provide a reasonable income. Some states provide a list of securities from which a trustee may choose.

quotation also known as **quote:** the highest bid to buy and the lowest offer to sell a security on the market. The quote tells you how your stock is doing.

record date: the date on which a stockholder must be registered on the stockbook of a company in order to still receive dividends in that quarter and to be able to vote on any company affairs.

red herring: See Index.

registered representative also known as **customer's man, account executive** or **customer's broker:** an employee working with securities who has met the requirements of the New York Stock Exchange regarding knowledge of the securities business.

registrar: the one in charge—such as a bank or trust company—of preventing the issuance of more stock than authorized by a company.

registration: procedure required by the Securities Act of 1933 that before new securities may be offered by a company, the securities must be registered.

regular way delivery: usual procedure on the New York Stock Exchange whereby, when securities are bought or sold, the money trasnfer and stock transfer are usually accomplished on the fifth business day after the transaction.

right(s): privilege of shareholders to buy additional securities in the company ahead of the general public and at a reduced price whenever the company wants to raise money. The stockholder has a certain number of rights per share which he or she may sell rather than use.

round lot: a unit of trading. In the New York Stock Exchange a unit is generally 100 shares. In some inactive stock the unit is 10 shares.

seller's option: right given by the New York Stock Exchange for the seller to deliver stocks or bonds any time within a specified period, which may range from not less than 6 business days to not more than 60 days.

short position: term for stocks sold short and not covered as of a certain date. On the New York Stock Exchange a tabulation is issued once a month listing all issues on the exchange in which there was a short position of 5,000 or more shares and issues in which the short position had changed by 2,000 or more shares in the preceding month. Short position also means the total amount of stock an individual has sold short and has not covered as of a particular date.

short selling also known as **short sales** or **short covering:** rather than shares being bought first and sold later, the practice whereby shares are sold first and bought later in expectation that the market will go down. The broker "borrows" the stocks, sells them and holds the funds from the sale as collateral. The borrowed stock must be replaced by buying an equivalent amount (short covering) at a later date. If the stock goes down it will cost less to replace and a profit is made. There is an interest on the loan and stockbroker commission. One can do this transaction with stocks one already owns. For example, Mary Smith owns 200 shares of ABC which she feels will temporarily go down. She decides to borrow 100 of her own shares to sell short. This is known as selling short against the box.

SIAC: abbr. of Securities Industry Automation Corporation. An independent branch of the New York and American Stock Exchanges which provides data processing, central clearing and communication services to the two exchanges.

sinking fund: See Index.

SIPC: abbr. of Securities Investor Protection Corporation which provides funds, when necessary, to protect member firms' customers' equity.

special bid: an order to buy an unusually large block of stocks such as for a pension fund. The sale is regulated by expedient procedures such as making the sale on the floor of the exchange at a fixed price which may not be lower than the last or current sale of the security. The seller does not pay the commission.

special offering: stock sale at a fixed price. The commission is included in the price. Allotments are made if there are more buyers than stock.

specialist: a member of the New York Stock Exchange who keeps track of the limited orders. If necessary, he buys and sells on his own account to maintain a balance of supply. He also executes and keeps a record of brokers' orders.

speculator: person willing to take risks, reasonable and not so reasonable, in the hope of making large gains.

split: agreement voted by the directors of the corporation and approved by its shareholders to divide the outstanding shares into a greater number of shares, such as 2 for

1; the equity remains the same. Ann Smith owns 100 shares of XZ stock selling for $50 a share. After the 2 for 1 split, Ann Smith owns 200 shares of XZ stock at $25 a share.

Standard and Poor's Stock Price Index: index similar to *Dow Jones Industrial Average*, except Standard and Poor uses not 30 industrial corporations, but 500 major corporations consisting of 425 industrials, 25 railroads, and 55 utilities, all listed on the New York Stock Exchange.

stock dividend: a dividend paid out in shares rather than cash. The shares may be of the issuing company or in a subsidiary of the issuing company.

stock exchange:

NYSE	New York Stock Exchange
BOX	Boston Stock Exchange
MID	Midwest Stock Exchange
MSE	Montreal Stock Exchange
PE	Philadelphia Stock Exchange
TSE	Toronto Stock Exchange
PSE	Pacific Stock Exchange
CBOE	Chicago Board of Options Exchange (the first auction market for calls on a select list of NYSE stocks)
AMEX	American Stock Exchange (trades stocks as well as options of NYSE-listed stocks)

stock option: the right to buy (*call*) or sell (*put*) stocks at a fixed amount, at a specified price within a given time.

1) A *single call option* gives the owner the right to buy 100 shares of a specific stock at a specific price (*striking*

price) at any time prior to the *expiration date*. The price of the option (also known as *premium*) is the cost per share with a minimum unit of 100. A quoted price of "one" means that one option on 100 shares of stock costs $100. Should the stock rise sufficiently to cover the cost of the premium before the expiration date, the owner will have made a profit. For example, XYZ stock costs $100 on the day Mary Smith takes an option for $10 to buy at that same price a month from now. XYZ rises to $200, but because Mary Smith contracted to buy at $100, she makes a profit of $100 less the premium she pays per share. In this case she has doubled her money. Had the stock gone down, she still would have had to pay the $100 and she would have lost the difference.

2) One can do the converse: contract to sell (put) a specific stock. Suppose Mary Smith felt her XYZ bought at $100 had a good chance of going down in price. She can contract to sell (put) at $100 on the due date. If XYZ goes down to $80 a share, Mary makes a profit of $20 a share. Should the stock go up, she would lose money.

3) One can buy (call) and sell (put) another option of the same company, this is known as *spread* or *straddle*. Spreads or straddles can be a convenient way of spreading the risk or switching out of one option and into another. Suppose Mary Smith had contracted to sell her XYZ stock and then realized that XYZ would have an excellent chance of actually going up in price. She could then straddle or spread her risk by putting in a separate call order due on another date.

Stock options can be bought and sold anytime prior to *expiration* date in much the same way as listed stock. The prices of the current stock options appear daily in the *Wall Street Journal* and many local newspapers. A summary of the week's trades appears in *Barron's.*

stock option contract: contract giving the purchaser the right to buy a number of shares of stock designated therein at a fixed price within a stated period of time.

stop limit order: *stop* is the price at which a person wants to buy or sell a stock or option; the special character is that the offer, if one is buying, is a price that is higher than the lowest offer; and, if one is selling, is lower than the highest bid. The buyer or seller is willing to do this because he or she feels the bid is ahead of the market's trend.

The *limit* is the least favorable price at which a buyer or seller will permit the order to be executed. For example, John Smith said he wished his stock to sell at 39, but was willing to take 35. The *stop* is 39 and the *limit* is 35.

stopped stock: a guarantee to receive a stock at a certain current price with an opportunity to buy at a slightly more advantageous price. Such an order is executed by the broker and the specialist. Mary H. wanted to have AB stock in her portfolio. The current price was 16½. Her broker asked the specialist to hold 100 shares at 16½, but should the stock go down to 16¼ (a savings of $25 for Mary H.), then the specialist would buy it at the lower price. Should the stock go up to 16½, Mary has her stock guaranteed at 16½.

street: Wall Street and the financial community immediately surrounding it.

street name: term for securities held in the broker's or brokerage firm's name and not in the customer's name. Sometimes customers prefer to have the stocks in the broker's name because, among many other reasons, they can be used as collateral when the customer wishes to buy on margin.

syndicate: a group of individuals and/or investment firms, banks and stockbrokers who are temporarily associated together under one manager for some specific business venture. For example, it may be to underwrite a particular security or to invest in a large real estate undertaking such as a shopping center or an office complex.

takeover: acquisition of one corporation by another. It may be friendly or incur a proxy fight. In order to win, the acquiring company may offer a higher price than warranted for the available stocks. (See *merger*.)

technical analysis: the practice of choosing the securities for one's portfolio not by how a corporation fares, but by the movement of the price of its stock.

tender offer: request by a corporation—under specific terms and for a certain time period—for the public, and other stockholders such as institutions, to surrender their stocks—usually at a price higher than the current market.

thin market: market condition whereby there are few bids to buy or sell on the market as a whole or in one specific stock or area.

third market: See *over-the-counter.*

time order: a limited price order at a specified time.

tip: supposedly inside information concerning the financial world.

top heavy: term describing a market priced too high (for sundry reasons) and likely to decline.

trader: one who buys and sells for short-term profit.

trading post: a term for each of the 23 different trading locations on the floor of the New York Stock Exchange at which stocks assigned to that post are bought and sold. Each post trades approximately 75 stocks.

treasury stock: stock issued by a corporation, reacquired by the corporation, and which may be held in the company's treasury. Such stocks have no voting rights and do not receive dividends.

turnover of working capital: within a given period, the amount of income in dollars produced by each dollar of net working capital.

underwriter: dealer or broker in an investment company who buys new issues from a corporation with the intent to resell these securities to the public.

unlisted: description of a security not listed on one of the exchanges and therefore sold over the counter. Today admission of a stock to unlisted trading privileges requires S.E.C. approval dependent on filed information.

up tick also known as **plus tick:** a transaction made at a price higher than the preceding transaction. A stock can only be sold short on an up tick. If stock trades at 20, then at 20½, it can be traded on the up tick. If it doesn't move and is traded again at 20½, it is a zero plus tick.

warrant: a certificate giving the holder the right to purchase securities at a stipulated price within a specified period of time, or sometimes perpetually.

wire house: larger member firm with many branches. Originally a wire house was a member firm of an exchange maintaining a communication network linking either its own branch offices, the offices of correspondent firms or a combination of such offices; today, because everyone has access to information and communication systems, the term has changed its meaning.

working control: ownership of at least 51% of a company's stock—the minimum amount that one must own to exercise control in the company.

COMMODITIES –

CDF: abbr. of commercial deposit futures. CDs are private debt instruments in which speculators buy futures. When money is tight rates rise. When money is available rates may decline.

commodities: products such as soybeans, sugar, gold, coffee, etc., which are traded at a price set in the future. If the commodity's future price is less than predicted, the purchaser loses money. Once the future contract has expired the trade is finished. The speculator either sells at the price or takes possession of the product. Commodities have no equity; the speculator buys only hope.

commodity cash market also known as **spot** or **actual market:** market for goods bought in large quantity for immediate delivery for actual use. For example, a chicken farm would buy chicken feed on a spot market. Cash prices are less than future prices because there are no insurance, storage or broker fees.

commodity exchanges: Chicago Board Of Trade is the largest commodity exchange in the world. Approximately 90 percent of the world's grain futures trading is handled on its floor. Corn, oats, rye, soybeans, live choice steers, iced boilers, silver and plywood are also traded. Other exchanges are in New York as well as in Minneapolis, Kansas City, New Orleans and in Winnipeg, Canada. Commodity exchanges are member organizations each with its own governing board which sees to it that business is carried out according to regulations. Nonmembers trade through brokerage firms which hold membership through partners or officers.

commodity futures contract: a promise to buy or sell a certain amount of goods at an agreed price at a fixed future date.

commodity futures market: buying and selling for future delivery; some buy to speculate and sell before delivery.

commodity futures maturity date: delivery date.

commodity margin: the amount the customers must pay. The cash requirements for commodities trading are low: 5–10 percent, varying according to the commodity and to the broker's standards. There are no interest payments on the balance.

commodity option: generally traded on the London market, commodity options are *calls* (to buy) and *puts* (to sell) on commodity futures contracts. The speculator cannot lose more than the cost of the options. A commodity option is the right, not the obligation, to buy or sell a futures contract, at a fixed price for a certain period of time. The option buyer has a known risk, usually 10 percent of the value of the goods covered by contract.

For example, John Smith buys 1 ounce of gold futures at $400 an ounce until next June. He says, "If you give me a premium (a *surplus*) of $40 I will give you the option (*choice*) of buying my contract at $600 an ounce." John Smith is betting that gold will not go as high as $600 so that the buyer will not claim it. If he is right, John Smith pockets the $40 (the *premium*) and keeps the future contract. If the price of gold does go to $600 (*into the money*), he at least gets to keep the $40 and the option buyer can buy the gold at $600 and take the $200 profit. If the option buyer loses, he is only out $40.

commodity option commissions: commissions smaller than in stocks and negotiated when there are more than 19 contracts involved.

commodity short sale: in principal, the same as in stocks (see *short selling*) except since commodities are for future delivery the commodity does not have to be borrowed from someone as in the stock market. Nor are there special up tick (see *up tick*) rules for going short, because if a short position is closed before the future date, no physical commodity delivery is required as with stocks.

commodity speculators: those that play the commodity market to make money and who accept the risk hedgers want to avoid by taking positions in the market. (See *hedge*.)

contract: agreement in a commodity trade that specifies the purchase price, quantity, date, and specified location; the minimum amount one can buy is one contract. The term comes from the early days when mainly agricultural products were traded and refers in part to the size it takes to fill a railroad car. Today one contract may mean 5,000 bushels of wheat or so many pounds of sugar. It may also refer to metals.

daily price limits: how much or in what point range the market may move up or down within one trading day. Limits exist for the protection of speculators and member firms of the exchange.

delivery date: the date the commodity bought should be delivered; on the commodity market, the day the future contract expires.

genuine risk capital: money that an investor can afford to speculate without risking his livelihood, standard of living, or family.

hedge: a means of preventing loss from price fluctuations; when a sale or a purchase is made involving a commodity, it is counterbalanced by a sale or purchase of the same commodity in the future.

intercrop straddle: the purchase of a future in one crop year as compared to the sale of a future in a different crop year.

intracrop straddle: the sale of one future sale versus the sale of another future within the same year.

long: to buy futures.

margin call: a request from the broker for more money

if a future declines below the standard set, usually 25 percent.

scale order: the order given by the trader to sell or buy commodities at intervals; a buy or sell order at regular price spreads of up or down to protect against loss. For example, 1,000 pounds of rice is bought at $1 a pound. If the futures go up ½ point, the order may be to sell half of the order then, and sell the other half when the future goes up another ½ point. This way the trader has made some profit at the first sale, so that if the price of rice should go down, the trader has some of the investment protected.

scalpers: those who buy and sell for a small price difference.

short: to sell futures.

spread: simultaneous purchase of a future for delivery in one month, and sale of a future in the same commodity for delivery in another month; a form of *arbitrage*.

stop order: an order to buy or sell a commodity contract above or below a given price. If corn is selling at $6 a bushel, a stop order to sell can be put in to sell if it goes down to $5.50, thus minimizing the loss.

straddle: Trade in two different markets, such as August oats and August corn.

straddle based on different stages of processing: purchase or sale of futures in equivalent quantities as, for example, December soybeans, soybean oil, soybean meal, etc.

zero-sum game: another term for future market. The commodity market has for every up position a down position—thus making it a zero-sum game. For example, oranges may be up and wheat down. Not to be compared to the stock market, which has as whole market up or down cycles.

MONEY – INSTRUMENTS

Agency Discount Notes: short-term loans to federal government agencies which are bought through a broker. Instead of receiving interest, the notes are bought for less than they will pay at maturity. For example, a $1,000 6-month note may be bought for $900.

annualized average yield: an investment firm's average interest rate earned within a given period. The yield depends on operating expenses as well as the type of investments chosen by the directors.

annuity: series of payments received in the future, most often from an insurance policy. Premiums are paid in a lump sum or in installments.

Average Maturity Index of Money Funds: a figure representing the average length of maturity in the present money fund industry. The index shows nothing more than how popular long-term and short-term notes are at the moment. If the maturity date is long it may mean money market fund managers are locking themselves into long maturities because they expect rates to drop; if the average maturity date is brief it means money market managers are seeking short-term funds because they expect the interest rates to rise. The index is in newspapers that list money fund yield tables.

banker's acceptance: a trade draft guaranteed by an accepting bank; the accepting bank is the one that guarantees payment for the goods.

certificate of deposit also known as **CD:** a receipt for a large sum of money placed in the bank which may bear interest and/or pay earnings at maturity. Banks today will let smaller accounts participate in CDs by "lending" them the additional money. The loan, of course, costs the client interest. CDs are insured by the Federal Deposit Insurance Corporation up to $100,000 per individual.

CMA: abbr. of Cash Management Account. The investors' money, which may come from stock dividends or bond interest, is placed in various liquid assets. The customer may also use stocks and bonds in the account as margin. All these assets—the cash in the margin account awaiting investment in the money market fund, the net asset value of the customer's investment in the money market fund, plus the total available loan value of the securities in the margin account—enable the customer to open a credit card and checking account affiliated to the CMA from which he or she can draw cash and/or obtain needed credit.

commercial banks also known as **full service:** nongovernmental banking institution designed to finance production, distribution, sale of goods, to lend short-term funds, provide credit cards, personal loans, foreign exchange, trusts, safe deposits, investment management, underwriting, and every other conceivable commercial function.

commercial paper: an IOU for large amounts of money issued by banks and corporations whenever they need money for the company's inventory fluctuations or other seasonal needs. These short term promissory notes are usually sold for a period of anywhere from 24 hours to 270 days. The maximum maturity permitted is 270 days. Investors in commercial papers tend to be other large companies who receive interest approximately equal to prime rate. The IOU usually has no collateral and is backed by the general reputation of the issuer.

credit union: agency that lends money at a more favorable rate than commercial institutions. Money saved by members is normally placed in share accounts and the earnings are divided and paid back as dividends to each shareholder. The Federal Credit Union Act was passed by Congress in 1934 "... to make more available to people of small means credit for provident purposes through a national system of cooperative credit...."

custodian bank: bank charged with safekeeping assets.

debt instrument: another term for loans and forms of money to serve debts.

discount rate: the rate the Federal Reserve Bank charges its member banks for borrowing money. The rate is indicative of the bank's cost of funds.

employee thrift plan: a voluntary regular savings plan for the benefit of employees in a company. The funds are invested to increase income. The employer or corporation may or may not add to the fund.

Eurodollar Certificate of Deposit: deposit of U.S. dollars in a foreign bank.

Eurodollars: deposits of U.S. dollars in banks and other financial institutions in Europe. The Eurodollar market dates from 1957. The decline in the use of sterling as an international currency was accompanied by an increased use of the dollar. Transactions take place outside the country whose currency is being dealt in, and the success of the market owes a great deal to the fact that it is outside the control of any national authority.

Euro Time deposit: passbook type of deposit in a foreign bank.

FDIC: abbr. of Federal Deposit Insurance Corporation, an independent agency in the federal government established to insure the deposits in all member banks.

federal reserve: a national bank clearing system whereby each member bank keeps a certain percentage of its money on deposit at the local Federal Reserve Bank. The reserve is lent each day to banks that may be short of funds that day. The interest rate charged is known as Federal Funds.

Federal Savings and Loan Insurance Corporation: an independent agency in the federal government which insures the savings accounts of participating banks up to a minimum amount.

IRA: abbr. of Individual Retirement Account. The Internal Revenue Service allows each person to take $2,000 annually tax-free from the top of his or her salary for the purpose of investing that money on a deferred tax basis until the minimum age of 59½.

liquidity: ability to convert investments to cash with no or minimum penalty.

money fund check account: account from which participants in the money fund are permitted to write checks to withdraw money in the amount equal to or exceeding the minimum amount indicated. The money in the fund keeps earning interest right up to the moment the checks are cleared.

money fund dividends: dividends which, in contrast to those from stocks, are declared daily and credited to each account, and in most cases are automatically reinvested in the fund.

money fund shares: the amount owned in a money fund. Usually a share is $1. The price per share always stays the same but the interest it earns fluctuates.

money market: a network of borrowers and lenders of money who operate out of brokerage houses, banks and private firms.

money market certificate: certificate for small amount of private money, usually in the sum of $10,000, which is pooled to lend large sums of money to corporations at higher than passbook interest rates. These certificates require in most cases a 6-month deposit and have severe penalty for early withdrawal. Money market certificates have been conceived, organized and permitted by the federal government only since June 1, 1978.

money market instrument: 1) a type of debt vehicle; 2) money owed with various types of repayment guarantees such as bank certificates, commercial papers, U.S. Treasury bills.

money market mutual fund: money pooled by many people for the purpose of investing in the money market; investments in lending instruments including U.S. Treasury obligations, U.S. Government agencies, certificate of deposit, banker's acceptances, commercial papers.

money market rating services: statisticians who keep track of money market funds' credit risks, rate risks and market risks. The best-known services in the field are Standard and Poor's, Moody's and Fitch.

money velocity: the speed with which money turns over.

municipal discount notes: See *municipal notes*.

National Association of Security Dealers: investment dealers' self-regulating organization.

no load: commission free; most money funds do not take a commission.

NOW accounts: free checking accounts which require at all times a minimum deposit. In return the bank will pay the account-holder interest on the money in the account. If the account drops below the minimum, the bank imposes a service charge.

participating out: a term used by banks for the sale or purchase of loans to adjust their capital position.

passbook savings: savings deposited in a bank. Interest rates are 5–5½ percent compounded. The passbook is given to the depositor; similar to a ledger, it records deposits, withdrawals, interest.

prime rate: See Index.

project notes: loans to local housing authorities which are guaranteed by the government and sold through a broker. Depending on the current interest rate, these loans may be at a discount, a premium, or at par value. (See *par bond*, *premium*, and *discount note*.)

REPOs: short for repurchase agreements. Bonds, notes or CDs are sometimes sold by a bank or investment house to another investment house with the privilege of repurchase. The repurchase agreement may include accrued interest and/or repurchase at a few points above the original selling price. These transactions are short term and fulfill the need for short-term liquidity without having to sell loan issues.

Savings and Loan Association also known as **Savings Association, Building and Loan Association,** and **Cooperative Banks:** association that accepts deposits from individuals and pools such funds for home loans. The public that places its money in such associations receives interest as well as contributes to the home lending function.

savings bank: institution classified as nonprofit which makes loans and pays dividends on depositors' savings accounts. Mutual savings banks are entitled to special nonprofit tax treatment.

savings club: savings accounts like Christmas club, vacation club, etc., set up with regularly required payments to serve as an incentive for the depositor to put money in the account. Interest rates are presently lower than in money funds. (See *passbook savings*.)

SSC: abbr. of small saver certificate. A major interest-bearing deposit available from banks; federal regulations place a heavy early-withdrawal penalty on such certificates.

STIF: abbr. of short-term investment fund. Investment opportunity offered by money managers to those with trust accounts that pools all their liquid funds and invests the money market. This allows those with income from stocks and bonds to earn day-to-day interest on their dividends until they are ready to use that money.

treasury securities: borrowings by the federal government from investors. (See *treasury bills*, *treasury notes*, and *U.S. Savings Bond.*)

unit investment trust: a mutual fund only sometimes available which invests in all types of securities such as bank CDs and Eurodollars. The fund is bought in units of $1,000, matures in 6 months, but may be sold anytime without a penalty; if interest rates go down, the unit goes up in value and sells at a profit. Unit Investment Trusts are set up to serve various purposes and some are tax-exempt investments.

DIAMONDS – AND PRECIOUS METALS

about uncirculated: a choice coin that has hardly been circulated.

American Gem Society: a professional society in the United States and Canada which awards titles to individuals and firms, sets business standards, and publishes and makes available a periodical and informative brochures.

American Gold Coin Exchange: a subsidiary of the American Stock Exchange (AMEX) which trades gold bullion coins: Canadian Maple leaf, South African Krugerrand, Austrian 100 Corona, and Mexican 50 pesos. The transaction to buy or sell is carried out for the customer by a broker.

ASA LTD.: South African–based closed-end mutual fund whose shares are traded on the New York Stock Exchange. Primarily invests in top 16 gold mining companies in South Africa.

assays certificate: a document of verification that the metal being purchased is pure and real.

base price (of pearls): the price of the particular pearls = the average size of the pearls in question × their total weight × the base rate.

blue white: label for a diamond with no color except a bluish tinge which contributes to value. Also known as *color*.

brilliant: a diamond cut with 58 facets, 33 at the front and 25 at the back of the girdle.

brilliant coin: gold or silver coin of exceptional luster.

Bureau of Mines: agency of U.S. Department of the Interior which, among other functions prepares a *Minerals Yearbook* for the U.S. Government Printing Office. The yearbook lists, describes, and reviews world prices and sources of metals and minerals.

certificate of deposits: receipt given for gold deposited with a goldsmith. Historians consider these certificates forerunners of money. (See *gold standard.*)

clarity: the degree to which a diamond is without flaw. Contributes to its value.

coin gradings: terms used to describe the general characteristics of coins. Included are

fair—quite worn
good—designs and date clear

very good—clear and bold features
fine—little wear
very fine—very little wear; all markings clear; rim smooth
extra fine—hardly circulated; top condition
uncirculated
proof—those coins struck for collectors; mirrorlike luster

color: See *blue white.*

COMEX: abbr. of New York Commodity Exchange. Trades futures in gold, silver, platinum, and copper.

costume jewelry: jewelry containing imitations of gems and metals and materials of little value. Designed for use with current fashion.

counter-cyclical metal: trends involving metals contrary to stock market trends, such as gold going down when the stock market goes up, and vice versa.

diamond: pure carbon, the hardest substance known to man; crystals found mostly in octahedron formation so rough they were not valued by the ancients until scientific cutting was developed. Considered by many as a hedge against inflation, wealth more easily portable than gold.

electronic metals: metals including antimony, germanium, indium, iridium and rhodium used in key laser components and other sophisticated technology.

Exchange Stabilization Fund: an agency within the U.S. Treasury Department which has more than $1 billion at its disposal to use as it sees fit to stabilize currencies.

Price of gold is indirectly linked to foreign exchange rates, especially the value of the dollar to other currencies.

extremely fine: label for a coin in which practically all intricate detail shows.

Federal Reserve Bank: warehouse agent for storing gold for central banks of the United States and foreign countries.

fine: label for a coin acceptable to collectors.

fine weight: total weight of the pure gold or silver in a gold piece.

fineness: the proportion of pure gold or silver in coins, jewelry, or bullion expressed in parts per thousand.

first water: pure white diamond that is free of flaws, which contributes to its high value.

14 karat gold: metal that is 14 parts gold, 10 parts alloy.

gem: cut and polished stone possessing durability and value; beautiful enough to use for jewelry.

gem coin (coin grading): flawless gold or silver coin.

gem material: any synthetic material that can be substituted for a real stone.

gem mineral: any mineral species which meets the qualifications of a gem and may thus be made into jewelry.

gold: oldest precious metal; it does not rust, tarnish, scale or decay.

gold and silver dealers: those who buy and sell and sometimes store gold and silver in coins or bullion for clients; includes banks, brokerage houses, and coin dealers.

gold bar: bar of gold in sizes from ¼ ounce to 400 ounces.

gold bullion: bars of gold in various weights and usually stored in bank vaults; their value is controlled by market price.

gold bullion coins: coins that vary in size and fluctuate with gold market price.

gold coin: a full troy ounce of pure gold in the shape of a coin. The value of a gold coin fluctuates with the current price of gold. Gold coins are easy to transport and store, and are considered a protection against the devaluation of money.

gold standard: gold as a monetary standard. Since gold is heavy to transport, nations who originally used gold as a monetary standard issued money. This money is actually considered as *certificates of deposit* for gold.

gross weight: total weight of a gold or silver piece including its alloys.

ingot: any metal cast into a bar or other shape.

junk silver: pre-1965 silver dimes, quarters and 50-cent pieces. These silver coins contain 90% silver and are traded in bags containing $1,000 in face value. The approximate value of these bags can be determined by multiplying 720 ounces times the current price of silver bullion.

karat: in the United States, the degree of fineness of solid gold.

key coins: in a series coin collection, those coins made popular by supply and demand; the most popular coin in a series.

leverage: a term used in coin collecting to describe the situation when a coin is in short supply and will therefore take a wide swing when there is a significant change in demand.

light metals: metals such as beryllium, magnesium, titanium, and their various alloys which are not sensitive to light, heat or electronic impulses; vital in space structures because of their light weight combined with toughness.

London Metal Exchange: marketplace that trades gold, silver, and other metals.

marking: the hallmark of an exchange-approved refiner on a bar of gold or silver.

medallion: gold coin which is not legal tender.

metal traders: professionals who make up the free market in metals. They trade in all the metals and are active in metal exchanges where the future of these metals are traded. Some traders are large firms which own metals as a hedge (see *hedging*) and which subsidize mines.

metals broker: agent who buys on the market for a client for a commission and other fees such as storage, insurance, and assays costs. The broker negotiates each individual purchase with one or more metal traders for the best price.

mintage: the number minted (manufactured) of any one coin. For example, Mexico's 50-peso Centenario's mintage was unlimited.

Mohs's Scale of Hardness: a universally used general standard of comparison in noting the hardness of a gem expressed by numbers from 10 to 1. A diamond, the hardest gem, is #10; talc, the softest, is #1.

natural placer gold: gold in its natural form as gold nuggets and dust.

New York Mercantile Exchange: exchange that trades futures in platinum and palladium, crude oil, heating oil and gasoline. Each petroleum product is traded for New York harbor or Gulf Coast (Texas) delivery.

numismatic coins: gold or silver coins minted long ago

and now enjoying added value because of their rarity and historic value; often considered works of art.

off-the-wall indicators: world and political occurrences that affect world gold and silver demand without having anything to do with supply and production.

1 grain (troy): .0648 grams.

1 gram: 15.43 grains (troy).

1 metric carat: .200 gram (1/5 gram). Europe, Latin America, and most other countries in the world except the United States and Canada use the metric system for weighing precious metals. The United States plans to replace the troy system with the metric measuring system sometime in the 1980s.

1 ounce (troy): 31.10 grams; 150 carats.

pearl: a stone found in oysters, valued in the highest rank of jewels although not as durable (hard) as crystal gems.

physical: a term to denote a cash payment and/or to receive a hard product such as gold coins or gold and silver bullion as opposed to receiving a certificate or stock.

poor man's gold: a term for silver because it is less expensive than gold but in many ways more volatile in upswings and downswings, which by and large follow those of gold.

precious metals: gold, silver and platinum. Metals with

special physical and chemical properties that enhance their value. Some buy them as a means of maintaining the value of their wealth, others for decorative materials. They also are used as industrial commodities.

precious stones: comparatively valuable gems such as diamonds, rubies, sapphires, emeralds and pearls.

premium: the cost above the metal value; gold bullion coins have a relatively low premium.

real gold prices: commercial demand; annual average U.S. dollar prices of gold as established in London afternoon fixings; deflated or inflated by the world consumer price index constructed by the International Monetary Fund.

seigniorage: difference between the cost of the metal plus minting expenses and the face value of the money coined.

sell off: a term used to denote that the price will go down because people are selling.

semiprecious stones: a term not welcomed by the jeweler because it refers to varieties other than diamond, ruby, sapphire, emerald, and pearl. A case in point is jade, which is not listed as precious, but considering its resale value, it should not be categorized as semiprecious either.

shekel: a gold ingot of 8⅓ grams; first used by the Babylonians about 2000 B.C.

silver: a metal with a high degree of luster and polish and the highest thermal and electric conductivity of any substance.

silver bar: bar of silver available in sizes from 1 ounce to 1,000 ounces.

Silver Institute, Inc.: a research-oriented institute made up of industrial consumers, producers, and dealers to industry. The address is:

1001 Connecticut Ave. N.W.
Washington, DC 20036

slackers: workers weighing, shifting, and shipping gold bars. (See *Federal Reserve Bank.*)

specific gravity: density of a gem. The simplest way to measure this is to place the gem in a measured cup of water and measure the water it displaces.

stockpiling funds: stocks of strategic metals and precious metals kept to provide raw material for production at a future date. The participating investor expects a better than average return when demand increases. Some public issues are made available by such corporations as Strategic Stockpile Corporation to provide investors with liquidity and to use the proceeds to purchase metals which the corporations hope will rise.

strategic metal fund: similar to a mutual fund; this has in its portfolio twenty or more strategic metals that are considered most attractive. Very few firms have such funds available. Among them are Strategic Materials Corporation, Bache Halsey Stuart and Comark Commodities.

strategic metals: metals used for defense including cobalt, platinum, molybdenum, iridium, iron, steel, nickel, lead, tin, and zinc.

Strategic Metals Corporation: a London-based firm known for accepting small orders for metals including strategic metals; provides warehousing, insurance, inspection and documentation services; also manages a strategic metals fund (similar to a mutual fund).

strategic metals mutual fund: a fund which buys and sells strategic and other metals for profit.

24 karat gold: purest form of gold.

uncirculated: label for a flawless coin (no bumps, perfect rim.)

U.S. gold coin: a coin from the gold standard days.

very fine: label for a coin where some intricate detail shows.

warehouse receipt: the title to the metal purchased and stored in a warehouse; usually includes (separately) assays certificates and insurance policy. The receipt is a negotiable instrument.

REAL – ESTATE

absentee owner: one who owns property either for pleasure or investment but does not reside upon it and may leave its management to others.

acceptance: a written and signed contract agreeing to certain terms and conditions of an offer.

accessory apartment: a rental apartment created within a private home.

act of God: See Index.

age-life depreciation: life expectancy of a building, assuming the property receives normal maintenance.

agency: the relationship between principal and agent to do certain acts on the principal's behalf in dealing with a third party.

agency form: the contract in writing between owner and agent. In real estate the form involves how the agent may act for the owner, the percentage he is to get of a sale price, and how many days after expiration of the contract the agent is to get his due if clients he introduced to the property decide to buy the property.

agent: an authorized person who represents and transacts business for another. In real estate an agent may act for another to sell, rent or buy to or from a third party.

air rights: the rights to the use of the open space above a property. It also includes the right *not* to build, thereby assuring that light and air to an adjacent building will not be blocked out. In large metropolitan cities, air rights are sold from adjacent properties.

amortization: See Index.

apartment house: 3 or more self-contained residential units in either a high-rise building or sprawling garden complex providing heat and water and complying with the residential laws.

appraisal: the application of analytical techniques to arrive at the value of a piece of real estate. Far from an exact science, appraisal involves the attempt to assemble pertinent data by methods of selective research in appropriate market areas.

appreciation: an increase in owner's equity.

arrears: payments due but unpaid; in real estate, usually refers to mortgage payments and/or a lien or property taxes.

assessed valuation: value of real estate upon which taxes are calculated.

assignment: transfer of title or interest in writing from one person or group of people to another. There may also be a legal transfer of mortgage (assignment of mortgage) or of contract.

assignment of lease: tenant's complete relinquishment of lease to another. Not to be confused with sublease, in which the leaseholder retains the lease and may even make a profit by renting the space at a higher sum than the lease stipulates.

assumption of mortgage: taking title to real estate that has an existing mortgage and assuming the responsibility for the existing mortgage.

attachment: See Index.

attractive nuisance: a hazardous condition maintained on one's premises because the owner does not recognize its danger. For example, a circus may have a caged lion on its property. However, if the cage is such that an unknowing child can actually reach in between the bars to touch the lion, the owner is maintaining a hazardous condition. The owner needs to add a fence or other railing to make it impossible for a child to touch the lion.

avigation easement: permission for aircraft to fly below a certain elevation. This is common for properties near or bordering airports.

backfill: earth that has been moved for such purpose as digging a foundation and is then returned to properly grade the property.

bad title: a title which because of its flaws is unacceptable to the purchaser.

badlands: useless land.

base rent: fixed minimum guaranteed rent in a commercial property lease.

basic rent: subsidized housing rent computed on the basis of a maximum subsidy.

bench mark: when surveying land, the mark on a permanent object to and from which elevation and other points can be referred.

betterment: an improvement that increases the value of the land. The term must be distinguished from those that only maintain value. For example, the heater in Carol Smith's apartment house broke down. She could maintain the value of her building by having the heater repaired or she could buy a new heating unit, thus making her building worth more.

binder also known as **earnest money:** a sum of money given in good faith by one wishing to purchase a piece of property. Upon acceptance, it becomes a bilateral contract until the legal contract is drawn up. The money is held in escrow by a trustworthy person such as a lawyer, agent or bank.

blighted area: a neighborhood deteriorated in value but not yet a slum.

bog: wetlands.

bona fide: done in good faith, without fraud.

capital expenditure: an accounting, an outlay representing improvement and additions which may be chargeable to property accounts.

capital gain: profit gained by a sale of real estate after adjusted expenses. The amount of the selling price above the acquisition price.

capitalization method: an attempt to calculate net profit by deducting estimated normal expenses from the amount of income the property should bring.

capitalize: to put cash into a project.

carryover clause: clause in an exclusive listing stipulating that the broker is protected for a specified time beyond the expiration date if someone who was shown the property when the listing was in force should later decide to buy the property.

caveat emptor: "Let the buyer beware." Concept that one buys at one's own risk after having examined the property.

closing costs: the costs incurred individually to the buyer of a piece of property as well as to the seller. In part these include escrow fees, lawyers' fees, title insurance, documentary stamps on deed, recording the mortgage and other items depending on the state and specific needs.

closing day also known as **"passing":** the day the agreement of sale is consummated. The buyer signs the mortgage, and other necessary formalities are concluded; title and deed are transferred to the new owner.

cluster developing: development in which buildings are built grouped close together in order to leave as much wide-open space as possible. Not all communities' zoning laws permit such an arrangement.

commercial acre: that portion of an acre of commercial development which is designated for sidewalks, streets, etc.

commercial property: income property zoned for such businesses as hotels, motels, office buildings, shopping centers, warehouses, apartment houses and parking lots. Not to be confused with industrial, agricultural, or residential zoning.

commission: the fee paid by the seller to a broker for transacting a sale. The fee is usually or should be decided upon before the agent begins his work. Brokers usually have minimum rates, but may be renegotiated before a bid is accepted if the sale is not as high as the original asking price. The broker may or may not agree to lower his commission.

common property: land for the use by the public at large, often including property belonging to another, such as oceanfront property.

community property: property owned jointly by husband and wife. Though laws vary from state to state, the term refers mostly to property obtained during the marriage.

condemnation: the exercise of eminent domain; setting apart land by the government for a particular use or purpose such as highways, military reservations, or other public exigency. If the land is in the hands of private owners, the government has to recompense the value and loss to the owners either in money or exchange of land.

conditional contract: contract stating that transfer of title is to take place when the conditions of the contract have been fulfilled. Until then the title remains in the seller's name. A common condition is that the contract can only be fulfilled if the buyer can obtain a mortgage.

condominium: individual ownership within a building. The ownership may be of an apartment or an office with a deed and title. The owner may do as he or she wishes with the area. It maybe leased, mortgaged, bought, sold. Taxes are paid independently by each owner. The common areas such as garden, halls, heating plants, garage, etc., are owned jointly and costs are shared.

contract: the document containing the conditions of the sale and transference of title of real property, drawn up in a valid manner containing all essential points to make the transaction binding.

conversion: the act of changing the use of real property, such as changing a rental apartment into condominiums, co-ops, or offices, or changing a large private home into a school.

conveyance: the act of transferring property from one person to another. A contract and a deed are each forms of conveyance. (See *contract* and *deed*.)

cooperative brokers also known as **co-brokers:** two or more brokers working together to sell land. Costs and commissions are shared.

cooperative building: building whose owners are stockholders in a corporation that owns the real estate. Each owner pays, depending on the size of his area, a fixed rate to cover operating costs, mortgage, and taxes. A cooperative may be owned in an office, apartment building, or industrial park. Not to be confused with co-ownership which refers to two or more persons jointly owning an asset.

covenant: an agreement written into a deed stipulating certain acts and uses. For example, a man who owns a mountain with a stream may stipulate that all those who buy land in the area may not use the stream water for watering horses, or that each landowner may have horses only for personal pleasure and not for commercial purposes.

deed: the legal document used on closing day to transfer real property from one owner to another. Contains an accurate description of the property being conveyed and is signed, witnessed, and carried out according to the laws of the particular state.

depreciation: the decline in value of property. Loss in market value may occur for many reasons: for example, deterioration of a neighborhood or an Act of God. Appraisers define depreciation as the difference between present market value and replacement cost.

developer: a person who, for profit, puts land to its best use by the construction of improvements upon it. The land may be subdivided into homes, shopping centers, industrial parks, apartment houses or recreational facilities.

development property: 1) property already explored and known to be suitable for further development of such resources as oil, gas, precious metals, etc. Because a certain amount of risk is involved, and because the investment may be beneficial to the needs of the country, the federal government sometimes allows tax benefits to the investor. 2) land ready to be developed into homesites or commercial property.

devise: real property given as a gift in a last will and testament. The person who receives the gift is known as the devisee; the one who bequeaths the property is known as the devisor.

diluvium: the erosion of land by water such as tides and the flow of rivers and streams.

easement: a limited right to use another's property temporarily or permanently. Allowing the electric company to place a pole is permanent; permitting a neighbor to cross one's land until a road is built is temporary.

emblement: that which the lessor may take from the land after a lease expires; for instance, a tenant farmer whose lease is up may take the crop after it matures.

eminent domain: the right of the state to expropriate private property for public use. It must be in the best interest of the public and just compensation must take place.

encroachment: an intrusion upon the property of another without consent as, for example, a wall or fence that protrudes beyond its property line. If no one objects, it may be adjudged an implied easement. Encroachments may be delt with in any sale contract.

encumbrance: a legal right or interest in land that diminishes its value. It may be a pending legal action, change of zoning, easement rights, or liens. This does not prevent the owner from selling the land as long as a title search is done to reveal such encumberances, and the buyer is willing to accept them.

escrow account: See *binder*.

estate taxes: those federal and state taxes paid upon the transfer of property from the deceased to heir and legatees. State taxes vary and multiple state taxation may occur if the deceased had more than one domicile in more than one state, and in states which do not have reciprocal exemption provisions in their laws.

eviction: the act of forcing a person out from a property. There are three forms of evictions: actual, constructive, and partial. *Actual* is a total physical dispossession from the property. *Constructive* occurs when the landlord shuts off water, heat, etc. *Partial* is the case when one in possession is denied of a portion of the leased premises.

exclusive right of sale: a written agreement employing a broker for a specific time to the exclusion of all others. If another broker or the owner should sell the property in question during this time, the exclusive agent still gets a commission. (See *open listing* and *carryover clause*.)

exploratory property: property in which investments have been made in hopes that experts will discover a natural resource such as oil, gas, metals, etc., which will make it valuable. Since no one knows for sure what the property contains until it is tested, such investments may be very risky. Because they are risky but may help to develop raw land, the government often allows tax benefits to the investor.

federal lands: lands owned by the federal government.

fee simple: complete and absolute ownership of land which makes it freely transferable and inheritable. Any limitations that exist do not result from the nature of the estate itself but are due to such controls as zoning, building codes, etc.

firm price: a quoted selling price from which the owner will not deviate either by negotiating or accepting anything less.

first right to buy also known as **first refusal:** the privilege given a person to buy or lease real estate before anyone else; the right to meet any offer.

freehold: an estate in real property without a time limitation; free and clear ownership.

front foot: the measurement of property frontage. Property fronting on a busy main street may be more valuable than property fronting a side street.

functional obsolescence: end result of a building outliving its usefulness because of inadequate electric wiring, outmoded elevator, etc., so that it cannot compete with more modern facilities.

general improvement: public improvement that benefits many property owners in an area but cannot be directly charged to property owners. Improvements may include sewers or power or telephone lines.

graduated rental lease also known as **step-up lease:** lease having a rent which commences at a fixed rate and increases at set intervals.

ground lease: a lease of land alone exclusive of any buildings on the ground.

heavy industry: a zoning classification permitting industry that may be noisy, cause air pollution and have other undesirable aspects.

hectare: metric measurement equal to 2.471 acres or 100 ares. One acre is 100 square meters. The prefix "hect" means "100 times"; thus hectare is 100 ares.

high rise: building higher than 6 stories.

high-water mark also known as **mean high water** and **shoreline:** dividing line between public and private property. The shoreline is determined by the high wash of the waves or by the vegetation line.

homestead: family home owned and occupied by husband, wife, or brother(s) or sister(s) protected by state laws against eviction by general creditors except in cases of a real estate tax lien or a mortgage lien directly involving the home.

hypothecation: the pledge of property as security for a debt without giving up possession of it.

improved land: land which has been enhanced and made either more livable by the addition of such amenities as roads, sewers, buildings, or bridges, or fit for farming by the installation of an irrigation system and water lines.

inclusive rent also known as **fixed, flat** or **gross lease:** rental arrangement that encompasses such charges as gas, electricity, heat, parking, etc.

income property: property purchased primarily for monetary return such as an apartment house or a shopping center.

incurable depreciation: property beyond repair or where remodeling would be uneconomical.

index lease: a lease that provides for adjustment of rent according to changes in a price index such as the Consumer Price Index.

innocent purchaser also known as **bona fide purchaser for value:** one who purchases real property without knowledge of secret claims of a prior purchaser. State statutes protect an innocent purchaser.

inspection: the act of reviewing a premise before concluding the closing contract. Title insurance companies will visit a premise to search for *easements* not shown in public records or for building improvements (added porches, terraces, etc.). The lender or mortgagor will do the same, as should the owner-to-be a day or so before closing. In another context a landlord will inspect a leased premise before the tenant evacuates it.

intrinsic value: underlying reason for which property may be chosen: the features and amenities the area has to offer. Often land speculators judge future sales according to how well an area will stand up to growth; for example, what is farmland today may be a boomtown tomorrow.

investment property: property bought for the sole purpose of bringing profit at some future date.

joint tenancy: ownership by two or more persons with rights of survivorship. Only one title exists. The death of one does not destroy the owning title; the survivor receives the decedent's share.

just compensation: court-determined amount a person is to receive for the taking of his or her property. (See *eminent domain.*)

land trust: trust where real estate is the only asset. (See *trust.*)

land use intensity: a series of density ratings regarding floor area, open space, living space, and recreation space. Zoning codes vary from area to area.

landlord: the owner of a leased premise.

lease: an agreement between a landlord and a lessor whereby the landlord grants the right of possession for a sum of rent and other obligations to the lessee (tenant), but retains the right to retake possession of the premises after the agreement has expired.

lease option: a lease containing a clause giving the tenant the right to purchase the property. There are many different and variable features to such leases; for example, some leases state that the rent may be deducted from the purchase price.

legal description: description of a piece of property based on field notes of a surveyor or civil engineer and including lot, block, subdivision's government survey, and metes and bounds (terminal points and angles, distances and compass direction). Such descriptions are required by mortgagors, title companies, deeds and other legal instruments dealing with land.

leverage: In real estate, the use of borrowed funds to buy real estate that will increase in value so that it can be sold, and the larger return from which will not only show a profit, but will also pay off the debt and other investment costs.

levy: to assess property and set the rate of taxation.

light and air: there are no natural rights to light and air, and a neighbor has a right to erect a structure obstructing light and air. Easements designating where a neighbor may and may not build can be obtained in writing.

listing: to register property for sale or rent with an agency; an agency's register of property available. In real estate parlance there are many kinds of agreements. (See *exclusive right of sale*.)

littoral land: property affected by the tide current because it borders on the sea or ocean.

maintenance fee: the cost levied against property owners to maintain a commonly owned complex such as a condominium. (See *condominium*.)

management agreement: a contract between the owner of income property and the individual or firm that will manage the property. The contract includes fees, scope of responsibility—such as for repairs—payment of expenses, and termination procedures.

marginal land: land of poor value because it has poor access, is too steep, etc.

market value: determination of what a piece of real property will sell for; arrived at following appraisal of similar sales in the area and allowing for sufficient time to find a buyer.

master deed or **lease:** a condominium's principal deed or lease together with a declaration submitted according to state law when registering the complex.

mineral rights: the right to subsurface profits. These rights are not automatic and must be included in the deed when land is purchased.

Mutual Water Company: company organized by and for water users in a given district in order to have water at a reasonable rate. The stock is purchased by the users. Such companies are usually formed when a large new development is built which can't hook up to the nearest town's water because of distance or size.

net lease: lease on which the lessee pays not only rent, but also maintenance and operating costs including taxes, insurance, utilities, and repairs. Such leases are popularly used by industries and commercial outfits. Landlords like them because they do not have the usual management problems.

net usable acre: portion of a property suitable for building. Building may be limited not only by terrain but also by local zoning laws.

nominee: one delegated to act in a limited sense for another party. For example, if a person wishes to buy property quietly or without revealing identity, a nominee might act for the actual buyer.

notice of assessment: document issued by the state or local taxing agency to the owner of real property specifying the assessed valuation of the property. The assessed value is not as high as the market value.

100 percent location: prime business property usually with a high traffic and pedestrian count; an area with highest rental prices.

open housing: housing free from discrimination based on sex, race, religion, color, or national origin.

open listing: a listing given to all brokers in the area. The one who sells the house for the seller earns the commission.

percentage lease: a lease used by businesses based on a percentage of the monthly or annual gross sales made on the premises. There are many types of percentage leases and they are especially popular with retail stores.

plat: map of a town, section or subdivision indicating boundaries of individual properties; shows blocks, sections, public easement and dates and scales. In most cases these maps can be found in the tax assessor's office at the town or city hall.

progress payments: payment to the builder of a condominium or house as the building proceeds. Final payments are made when the buyer is satisfied that the work is completed according to specifications. Such arrangements are usually made in conjunction with a lawyer and a lending institution.

property income: monies from rents after expenses have been paid.

property report: a document required by law in interstate sales that covers important matters such as topography, soil conditions, schools, special costs, etc. If not submitted to the buyer at least 48 hours before closing, the buyer may cancel the sale.

proprietary lease: the lease an owner of a cooperative apartment signs with the corporation that sold him his shares in the building.

raw land: land in its natural state.

real estate: the earth below, above and at level grade with or without structures, trees and water.

real-estate option: to keep open an offer for a limited and agreed-upon time to buy or sell real property. Such an agreement may give a developer time to check out zoning laws, or it may give a person wishing to buy a private house time to resolve financial questions.

real-estate syndicate: multiple ownership of a piece of real property for the purpose of investment. Some participants may assume a passive role and only supply the capital, while others in the group may market and manage the property.

realtor: member of state and local real-estate boards affiliated with the National Association of Realtors. A realtor is a professional governed by the rules and regulations of the National Association of Realtors.

registrar: the person in charge of the records of all deeds, mortgages and other real-estate titles.

regression also known as **over-improvement:** a term to denote that when two adjacent properties are dissimilar the worth of the better property is lessened. For example, Mary and John Smith own a 4-bedroom house with a swimming pool on a block where all the other houses are 2-bedroom, 2-family houses. Mary and John will not get as much for their house if they decide to sell as they would if the same house were in a differently zoned block. Because of the nature of the neighborhood, the addition of the pool and the 2 bedrooms was *over-improvement* of the property.

REIT: abbr. of Real-Estate Investment Trust. Similar to an investment company, but concentrates its holdings in real-estate investments.

reliction: gradual recession of water from land, and therefore an increase of the land. Such uncovered land belongs to the owner of the property touching the border of the water.

REMT: abbr. of Real-Estate Mortgage Trust. Similar to an investment company, except that the mortgage trust buys and sells at a profit real-estate mortgages rather than real property.

rent: fixed-period payments made to the owner of a premise in return for occupancy with certain conditions and agreements.

rent control: regulations by state and local governmental agencies restricting the amount of rent landlords can charge their tenants. Rent control is only needed when there is an imbalance of supply and demand.

rental pool: agreement by participating owners of condominiums to have their units available for rental with a rental agent, and to share in the profits and losses of all rental apartments in the pool as agreed upon. Such pools are especially popular in resort areas where the owners only use their condominiums as a second home.

right of way: a privilege acquired by either usage or contract to pass over another's property. Tom Field owned a farm of several hundred acres, and the railroad had a right of way to build tracks on part of his property. Mary Smith bought raw land several hundred yards from the road; her deed included an easement that she may not be cut off from the road.

riparian: literally means riverbank and refers to the rights and obligations of ownership of land adjacent to or abutting on streams and lakes. Some riparian rights are swimming, boating, fishing, etc.

royalty: the sum paid to owners of realty for the privilege of depleting the property of its natural resources such as oil, gas, timber, gravel, or builder's sand.

run with the land: covenants which bind successive owners of a property.

sale-leaseback: a financing device whereby a developer sells his land to an investor (to get cash) and then leases it back under a long-term net lease. There are many variations and tax implications to this type of transaction which must be thoroughly studied before entering into such an arrangement.

security deposit: money deposited by or for the tenant with the landlord to protect the landlord against damages, failure to pay rent, and other problems. State laws vary on the interpretation of its uses and each lease should state the interpretation. For example, some security deposits are deposited in an interest-paying account and the interest is paid to the tenant.

separate property: property held individually, as opposed to community property. (See *joint tenancy*.)

special assessment: taxes levied for the cost of specific local improvements such as sewers, irrigation, drainage, and streets, to be paid only by those owners who will benefit by it.

spot survey: depiction of property and all its buildings under appraisal as well as those on any neighboring property that may encroach on the surveyed property.

spot zoning: a variance in the zoning law to permit change in a small area in a generally larger area, such as a 2-family house in an area zoned only for single houses. As a rule, must be court approved.

squatter rights: "actual, open, notorious, exclusive and continuous" possession to obtain rights to land when occupation is deemed untitled. State laws vary as to what amount of time (5, 7, 20 years) land must be occupied.

straw man: one who purchases property for another in order to conceal the identity of the real purchaser.

subdivision: any land divided into two or more lots for the purpose of disposition.

subject to mortgage: See *conditional contract*.

sublease: permission by a leaseholder for a third party to occupy rented premises for the whole term or part of it, usually for a higher price than the lessee is paying the landlord. Some leases contain clauses prohibiting subletting. The lessee always pays the landlord and collects directly from the third party.

survey: on-site measurement of lot lines, dimensions and positions of house or houses in a lot including any *encroachment* or *easement*.

syndicate: See Index.

tenant: the one who holds a lease.

tideland: land between high and low tides that is covered and uncovered by the ebb and flow of the tides.

time sharing: purchase or lease by multiple purchasers of a partial interest in a property (usually in a resort), giving them the right to use the facility for a fixed or variable time period each year. The cost is prorated among the owners.

title: lawful ownership to the property in question.

title insurance: protection for the property-owner against a forged deed or anything else that may have happened in the past to make the title worthless.

title search: an examination of the public records to trace the successive titles to the specific property up to the present owner. The search should prove the title to be marketable, clear and not defective in any way.

torrens: a systematic way of registering titles to speed up title search and proof of ownership.

trust: property, securities, and other financial holdings held and administered for the benefit of another.

turnover of working capital: in a given period, income in dollars produced by each dollar of net working capital; calculated when buying raw land or other real estate for investment.

undivided interest also known as **undivided right:** rights of joint owners in a property that cannot be separated from the other owners; tenants in common also have rights that cannot be separated from the other tenants.

undulating land: gentle sloping property; elevation changes of 3–8 percent.

unearned increment: an increase in property value not because of the owner's skill or efforts, but rather because of population increase, new zoning laws, the unexpected building of a nearby airport, etc.

unencumbered property: real property free and clear of mortgages, liens and assessment of any kind.

usufruct: the right to enjoy and profit from a particular property even though one does not own it. (See *easement*.)

variance: an exception made to the zoning laws. Permission must be obtained from the court. For example, a variance might be made in a residential area to permit a small, much-needed grocery store.

wasteland: land unfit for cultivation or development such as lowland or desert.

LOANS – AND MORTGAGES

add-on: a method used in installment loans in which the interest is added to the principal at the outset of the loan. The borrower receives only the principal requested, but pays back the larger sum of principal plus interest.

advice: acknowledgment in a form letter to a customer from a bank indicating that it has executed the instructions of its customer such as to make a transfer or a payment or to credit or receive money, checks, drafts, securities, or other documents. A bank also receives incoming or returning advices from correspondent banks.

amortization: a principal payment in reduction of a debt. The most common is a fully amortized loan, which is the gradual payment of the mortgage in periodic amounts until the total amount including interest is paid off. Amortization tables are available which show how much of the monthly payment is interest and how much principal. As the loan becomes smaller, the principal part of payment becomes larger, and the interest smaller.

annual percentage rate (APR): cost of a loan figured on the amount of credit advanced as well as the amount of time the money is used.

arrears: behind either in paying a debt or taxes, or in work such as construction that is overdue and incomplete.

assets: possessions that have monetary value.

attachment: taking a debtor's property into legal custody.

balance: amount of loan left to pay off.

balloon payment: the full and final amount that must be paid in one lump sum at the end of a loan. (See *balloon mortgage*.)

bankruptcy: inability to pay one's obligations so that creditors acting through the federal court and its trustee may seize available assets.

business loan: usually short-term credit or money loan so that inventory purchases may be made, equipment purchased, or short-term money needs met. (See *capital*.)

carrying charges: 1) the cost of carrying a debt; the fee asked by a store or other lender such as a credit card company for the privilege of charging goods beyond the bill's usual due date (loans); 2) costs incurred in owning property up to the time the development of the property is completed; this includes taxes and interest on loans (mortgages).

character: moral risk involved in negotiating credit or a partnership. Considered are: reputation for business honesty, promptness in paying obligations, standing in community, business record (successes, bankruptcies, and failures), reputation of business associates and habits such as gambling. Also considered are fire record, police record, civil court record, and general business ethics such as honoring contracts, employing unfair competition, or circulation of false rumors.

charge-off: a loan declared a loss because it cannot be collected.

chattel mortgage: term for personal, movable property such as automobiles, furniture, appliances; can be put up as security in a loan and be used as payment of a bad debt.

collateral: any asset such as securities, real estate, movable personal property, or life insurance used as a pledge for a loan.

consolidated loan: a new loan taken out to combine several debts so that only one large debt has to be paid off.

consumer credit: personal loans to individuals and families for personal use such as vacations or purchases, as opposed to loans for business or investment purposes.

cosigner: jointly guaranteed loan of which only one signer has the use of the money. (See *hypothecation*.)

credit card: a device which upon presentation obtains

credit for the holder of the card; according to the U.S. Congress, "'credit card' means any card, plate, coupon book, or other single credit device existing for the purpose of being used from time to time upon presentation to obtain money, property, labor or services on credit."

credit information: data obtained from reliable sources to evaluate credit worthiness. There are numerous sources from which to obtain information. Three frequently used sources are: 1) credit clearing house, also known as credit interchange bureau, which supplies information on a cooperative basis; 2) National Association Of Credit Men, a nonprofit, nationwide system of bureaus and districts which exchange credit information with each other. The association will provide a summary of all others' experiences with the account in question without revealing individual tradespeople's names; 3) credit investigator, also known as credit reporter, who may work for a bank, mercantile agency, commercial paper house, or business firm, and whose sources of information may come from credit files, banks, stores, and credit interchange bureaus as well as personal interviews.

credit line: the amount of credit a bank, lending institution, or trade firm will extend to a customer. Very often the customer is unaware of his own credit limit.

creditor: according to law, someone who regularly extends or arranges for credit which is repayable by agreement in more than four installments and/or for which payment of a finance charge may be required. For example, Mary Jones, who is a dentist, was told by one of her patients that she will have to pay Dr. Jones in three installments. Dr. Jones agreed and so is not considered a creditor in the legal sense.

deadbeat: slang for a poor credit risk.

deed of trust: deed to real property given by a borrower as collateral for a debt. A third person (trustee) holds the instrument of ownership for the lender as well as the borrower. If the debt is not paid off, the trustee may sell the property at a public sale; this procedure varies from state to state.

default: failure to comply with conditions such as payments due in a deed of trust or mortgage.

delinquent: past due, as in a loan payment.

dollar cost: the amount credit costs; the added cost of borrowing in order to buy property or merchandise.

drop dead fee also known as **commitment fee:** a kill fee to be paid when a borrower asks banks and other lenders to rapidly organize large sums of funds (in denominations of hundred thousands, millions and even billions) and then does not after all borrow the money. The borrower of such large sums is usually a corporation.

due date: the date an installment payment must be made or the date the final payment is made on a loan.

Equal Credit Opportunity Act also known as **Title VII to the Truth in Lending Act:** legislation passed in 1975 by the U.S. Congress making it unlawful for any creditor to discriminate against any applicant on the basis of sex or marital status with respect to credit transactions.

Fair Credit Reporting Act also known as **Consumer Credit Protection Act:** legislation that regulates the purpose for which a consumer reporting agency may provide a consumer report and limits what may be contained in it. If a person is denied credit or employment on the basis of a reporting agency's report, the person must be informed of this and given the name of the credit agency. If the consumer feels cheated, the act provides recourse whereby the consumer can defend him or herself.

Federal Land Bank System: a government agency which makes available long-term mortgages to farmers, enabling them to own their own farms. This agency is the largest holder of farm mortgages in the world.

finance charges: the full charges of a loan including not only interest cost but also fees, service charges, points, and investigation costs.

finance company: state-regulated, licensed and bonded consumer loan company.

financial adviser: an expert who advises individuals or families on all their holdings, investments and sometimes personal budgeting, accounting, estate planning, and taxes.

flat rate on unpaid balance: rate set on a daily or monthly basis for unpaid bills, used mainly by all types of consumer stores and credit card issuers.

forced sale: the sale of property by owner under duress; usually to satisfy unpaid taxes or liens.

foreclosure: a legal action to end all rights and possession of the mortgagor because of default in the terms of the mortgage by the mortgagor; the property then becomes the possession of the mortgagee or guarantor.

foreign correspondent: a bank in a foreign country acting and maintaining money for a domestic bank.

garnishment: a legal process by which a portion of the wages or salary of a debtor may be withheld by an employer for payment of debts.

grace period: the short time within which a past-due debt such as a mortgage may still be paid without penalty or default.

guarantor: one who pledges to pay a debt for another if necessary.

hangout: a long-term loan that exceeds the term of a lease for the same property. For example, John Smith built a factory for Mass Bakery Co., which signed a lease for 10 years. John Smith's mortgage was for 15 years with the stipulation that John Smith was to pay the balance of the loan if Mass Bakery did not renew its lease. (See *balloon mortgage*.)

hypothecation: the pledge of one's securities or property as a guarantee for a loan for another person or individual.

installment loan: a loan paid back in regular monthly amounts over a specified time.

installment plan: method of buying merchandise on extended credit whereby interest is added on to the unpaid principal and a contract is signed outlining the cost to borrow and how much is to be paid monthly. Usually the merchandise stays in the seller's name until it is paid off.

interest: See Index.

interest rate: 1) simple: the cost of borrowing money; percentage charged on a principal sum of money to pay for borrowing that principal amount; 2) compound: interest calculated upon the principal plus old interest due; 3) discount: interest paid in advance. For example, 10 percent discount interest results in a $1,000 loan owed but only $900 given to the borrower.

late charge: the penalty for failure to pay a regular mortgage or other loan installment.

letter of credit: a letter by a bank on behalf of its client authorizing another bank to make payments or accept drafts when the client has complied with all stipulations in the letter. The client guarantees payment to the bank issuing credit. For example, Carol Martin has a boutique in Cleveland and she needs to go on a buying trip to Italy. Her home bank knows that the boutique can afford to buy $25,000 worth of new merchandise, and issues a letter of credit for that sum on behalf of Carol Martin to their correspondent bank in Italy.

The bank in Italy will pay the wholesaler (also known as the beneficiary or 4th party) within the specified amount once Ms. Martin presents her bills to the Italian bank.

lien: a claim on property until a debt is discharged.

loan assignment: transfer of a claim, right, or property of a borrower to a trusted person who then is in charge of whatever has been transferred.

loan shark: unlicensed lender who charges much higher rates than licensed lending institutions, and will sometimes only accept full payment so that the high rates may be charged on the full amount right to the last day.

loan-to-value ratio: the ratio of a mortgage loan to the property's appraised value or its sale price (whichever is lower), and depending on the lending institution's policy.

luxury assets: any items such as boats or vacation homes not needed for income or living necessities, but which may be used as collateral as well as have a value when liquidated.

maturity: the date a mortgage note becomes due (See *balloon payment* and *balloon mortgage*), or the date the final payment causes it to expire.

mortgage: a long-term recorded note securing the debt that provides cash with which to buy real property. Upon full payment, the note will be cancelled. The property is always in the name of the mortgagor and not the lender. The property legally described is the lender's security in case of default, at which time the property may be sold and the debt satisfied with any additional money realized from the sale going to the mortgagor (providing there are no other debts).

There are many different types of mortgages, among which are the following:

amortized mortgage: debt that is paid off in equal amounts periodically over a predetermined span of time until the total amount, along with interest, if any, has been completely satisfied. (See *amortization*.)

ARM: abbr. of Adjustable Rate Mortgage, a new mortgage concept with many variables. The interest is adjusted periodically based on a specific index. Usually the rate has minimums and maximums. The main idea is similar to Variable Amortization Mortgage, except that the increase or decrease in the rate would not be added or subtracted to the monthly payment due, but instead the term (length) of the loan would be extended to a maximum of 40 years. Another method is to increase the outstanding principal (negative amortization) so that when the property is sold, the owner's equity is less than it otherwise would be. (See *amortization* and *variable amortization mortgage*.)

assumable mortgage also know as **assumption of mortgage:** the taking on of complete responsibility for an existing mortgage by the purchaser of a property, thus releasing the original mortgagor. (These mortgages are hard to find because as interest rates started to go up, banks refused to issue assumable mortgages.)

balloon mortgage: specified and periodic installments of principal and interest that do not fully amortize the loan. The final balance is due in a lump sum at a specified date in the future. (See *mortgage*.)

blanket mortgage: a mortgage covering more than one piece of property.

buy down mortgage: the agreement by someone other than the mortgage holder—such as the builder of a house or a developer—to pay part of the interest for the first few years of the loan. The builder can afford to do this by including the "cost" of his share of the loan in the sale price of the house. A builder may offer the arrangement as an incentive in order to sell houses that would otherwise be slow moving due to market conditions.

closed mortgage: a mortgage where no further advances are provided by the lender.

Federal Housing Agency (FHA) mortgage: mortgage provided by a lending institution that obtains insurance from FHA, a federal agency; the mortgagor pays FHA an annual insurance premium against default.

first mortgage also known as **first loan** and **first lien:** the mortgage that is superior, takes precedent to any other in case of default. It will be the first mortgage debt paid.

fixed rate mortgage: mortgage in which interest and principal payments are a constant and level amount.

floating rate mortgage also known as **variable rate mortgage:** loan for which the interest rate is not fixed, but moves up or down on the basis of indexes such as prime rate, treasury bills. Banks, savings, and other lending institutions reason that as interest rates rise, lenders can use the additional interest to pay dividends on new high-cost savings deposits such as 6-month money market certificates. This additional interest could, in turn, generate more loans for home buyers.

general mortgage: See *blanket mortgage*.

graduated mortgage payment (GPM) also known as **flexible rate mortgage:** conceived originally by the Department of Housing and Urban Development but used today by other lending institutions, the GPM provides for below-market payments during the early years; the differential is added to the principal of the mortgage, and at a specified date, mortgage payments are increased to the then current market rate.

hard money mortgage: a loan, often in the form of a second mortgage, for cash rather than to buy or maintain real estate.

junior mortgage also known as **second mortgage:** any mortgage such as a second mortgage subordinate in lien priority to a prior existing mortgage on the same property. John Smith has a mortgage on his house. He takes out a second mortgage. Should John default, his house will be sold. The cash from the sale will be used to pay off the first mortgage, and only what is left will be used to satisfy the second mortgage.

level payment mortgage: a mortgage repaid in equal periodic payments. (See *amortization*.)

open mortgage: 1) loan that may be repaid in full anytime without penalty; 2) mortgage that is past maturity date and interest rates are continued.

open-end mortgage: a mortgage that secures not only the original note and debt to buy the property, but any additional advance the mortgagee may choose to make in the future for additions such as a playroom, a garage, etc. The costs of executing a new mortgage are thus avoided.

package mortgage: a loan that finances not only the purchase of a house, but also personal items such as specified large appliances.

purchase money mortgage: a mortgage taken back by the seller to be paid off by the buyer as part of the purchase price.

reverse mortgage loan: a loan sought mostly by older people who own their home and wish to increase their retirement income. A new mortgage loan is taken out and given in monthly installments by the lender to the mortgagee over a period of years. Each payment is added to the unpaid principal amount. Settlement of the loan is made when the estate of the family sells the house.

rollover mortgage: one that replaces an existing mortgage and is "rolled over" for additional financing.

SAM: abbr. of Shared Appreciation Mortgage. The borrower obtains the mortgage at a favorable interest rate and agrees, in exchange, to share the profits with the lender when the house is sold. If the house is not sold within a given time, the lender may refinance the outstanding principal at current interest rates.

split financing: practice used by developers and investors whereby financing for land and improvements are arranged separately; allows a greater amount of money for a longer period.

spot loan: a loan to a particular property, usually a condominium unit, by a lender who has not financed the property.

spreader agreement: extension of a mortgage lien to encompass other property owned by the borrower in order to give the lender greater security.

standing mortgage: interest-only mortgage; principal is paid off at maturity. Not to be confused with *balloon mortgage*.

straight mortgage: a loan in which only interest payments are made periodically with the entire principal amount becoming due at maturity.

subsidized mortgage: monetary grant by the federal government as well as guarantees by the government to facilitate mortgage arrangements for a necessary real-estate project.

V.A. mortgage: a guaranteed loan made to an eligible veteran for the purchase or construction of a home with a small down payment or none at all.

variable amortization mortgage: a loan in which the principal does not initially have to be amortized or may be stepped up or down during the loan term. The rate of interest on the unpaid principal remains the same, while the amount of interest that must be paid will differ as the outstanding principal is reduced.

wrap-around mortgage: the combination of an original mortgage (retained usually because of a lower interest rate) and an additional mortgage (usually at a higher interest rate), becoming the junior mortgage. (See *junior mortgage*.) The entire loan (both mortgages) are treated as a single loan.

mortgage lien: a recorded instrument encumbering the property, and thus securing the underlying debt obligation. Because the lien is recorded, it receives priority over other obligations, provided it is a first lien. (See *junior mortgage*.)

overdraft loan: overdraft on a checking account allowed by certain banks with special arrangements. The overdraft is treated as a loan.

personal loan also known as **signature loan:** loan secured by an individual who may have a cosigner. (See *cosigner*.)

personal security also known as **personal guarantee:** guarantor for another person's debt. While the financial worth of the guarantor is taken into consideration, there is no specific pledge of collateral.

plastic money: term for credit card.

points: percentages of the face of the loan; for instance,

2½ points on a $100,000 mortgage would be $2,500 payable to the lender on the closing of the loan.

prepayment penalty: a charge by the lender when a mortgage is repaid before maturity; a means to recoup a portion of interest that the lender had planned to earn when the loan was made. Many people seeking a mortgage try to avoid such a clause.

prepayment privilege: the right to pay off without penalty a part or all of a mortgage.

prime rate: the lending rate charged for loans which are considered as less risky; loans to those customers who are considered as the bank's prime clients; rates higher than prime rate have "added premium" for risk.

principal: the money amount exclusive of interest; the money amount upon which interest is charged.

private mortgage insurance: a special form of insurance whereby a private insurance company guarantees the loan and thereby permits the lender to issue a much higher mortgage—in some cases as high as 95 percent of the purchase price. It is the same service as that of the Federal Housing Agency, except the insurance is provided by private firms.

promissory note: literally a promise by the borrower to repay according to specified terms the amount borrowed plus any other charges, fees, and interest. Such notes are popular when raw land is purchased; the buyer may ask the seller to let the land be paid off in ten annual payments with the land being purchased used as collateral.

quit claim deed: a release of deed which releases whatever interest the grantor has in the property. Mary Smith bought some raw land as an investment for $20,000. She paid $10,000 and gave the man who sold her the land a promissory note to pay $2,000 principal plus interest for the next five years, and in return, the land just purchased would be her collateral. When Mary Smith made her final payment on the promissory note, she received a quit claim deed from the person from whom she had purchased the land and who held the promissory note. The grantor "quit" whatever "claim" he had on the land.

rebate: the portion of the interest rate returned to the borrower when a loan is paid off early.

refinance: to obtain a loan to pay off another loan. This is done for several reasons, one of which is to generate additional capital to buy more property. Or, when interest on a particular mortgage is higher than the present rate, it is prudent to pay off the mortgage and arrange for a new one.

Regulation U: the term used for the Federal Reserve System's rules governing the extension of credit by banks on collateral loans; among other questions, the federal government asks what is the "purpose of the loan" and the ratings of any stocks and bonds used as collateral.

release clause: a clause found in promissory notes and mortgages usually involving raw land or development property. As a stipulated portion is paid off, a designated amount of land is released for sale.

repossession: the act of taking back goods purchased on the installment plan (see *installment loan*) because the buyer has fallen behind in the periodic payments.

revolving account: an agreement with a store as to the maximum amount one can owe at any time; interest is charged for the credit.

right of rescission also known as **"cooling-off" period:** provision of federal and some state laws allowing a purchaser to cancel a contract to purchase within a given time; the law was passed to help those who may have given in to high sales pressures when they really could not afford and did not wish to purchase the item.

satisfaction of mortgage: a certificate stating that a mortgage has been paid in full; must be recorded in order to be discharged of record.

secured loan: loan secured by securities, passbook, life insurance or goods such as a car which can become the property of the lender in case of default. Such loans may charge a lower interest because of their excellent security.

security: asset given as a pledge of repayment of a loan in case of default.

service charge: the fee apart from the interest paid on a loan.

simple annual interest: interest computed on the original principal and paid at the end of a year's use of the money.

single payment loan: a loan paid back in one lump sum; may be 1) a demand loan paid at the request of the lender or 2) a time loan with a set date of repayment for the whole amount specified.

Small Business Administration loan: an investment, SBA loans are those funds lent to small businesses by banks, and guaranteed by the U.S. government.

soft money: a term to denote carrying charges.

special lien: a charge against a specific property or parcel of land such as a mortgage lien. A general lien is a charge against all the property of the debtor.

subordination agreement: agreement by a prior mortgagee to become the junior mortgagee so that another existing or anticipated lien may be taken on. Such agreements are frequently used in development projects where a bank or other lending institution may refuse to lend money for construction unless it has the first mortgage position.

tax lien: a term for taxes due.

term loan: any loan with a maturity over one year.

term of the loan: length of the loan in months, days, or years.

tight money: money and credit that is scarce and/or expensive.

time contract: agreement stipulating periodic payments calculated to clear the debt by a specified maturity date.

Truth In Lending Act: a federal law regulating credit and protecting the consumer; the law requires that those seeking consumer credit be given clear, meaningful information about its cost; regulates certain credit advertising, certain credit transactions involving real estate, issuance of credit cards with limitations on the cardholder's liability for unauthorized use; designed to assist consumers in resolving credit billing disputes.

usury: the practice of charging an excessive amount of interest charging more interest than the legal rate.

INSURANCE –

accelerated option: a provision in a life insurance policy whereby the policyholder may use the policy's cash value and accumulated dividends to pay up the policy sooner than normal.

accommodation line: insurance business accepted by an insurance company from an agent that would have been rejected under normal circumstances but which is taken because of the agent's or customer's overall large account.

act of God: an occurrence such as flood, hurricane, earthquake, tornado or blizzard; not created by or under the control of human beings.

actual cash value (ACV): a term used in the settlement of damage to personal items and property; the value of an item equal to the original cost minus depreciation.

actuary: specialist trained in statistics and accounting who computes statistical tables relating to insurance; also computes premiums to be charged based upon the actual amount of paid claims in a given time plus the insurance company's operating costs.

adjuster: person who investigates a claim so that the claim will be settled by the insurance company; the adjuster may represent the insurance company or the policyholder.

age change: the date on which, for insurance purposes a person's age changes are noted. Such date is important in life and health insurance.

agency: person(s) known as agent(s) acting as an intermediary between insurance companies and the public. A *direct* agency represents only one insurance company and may be staffed by the insurance company; an *independent* agency represents many insurance companies.

aggregate limit also known as **excess of loss reinsurance** or **stop loss reinsurance:** a predetermined dollar amount during a specific period, usually 12 months, over which an insurance company is not liable; the maximum amount may be determined by a percentage of the company's premiums (loss ratio) for that period.

agreed amount policy: predetermined value of the insured item (rather than at the time of a claim).

aleatory contract: a contract depending on uncertain events, and in which both parties realize that one party may obtain for greater value under the agreement than the other.

all risk: coverage provided for all types of physical damage except those specifically excluded. Gradual deterioration from vermin, rust, etc., is usually excluded.

American Society of Chartered Life Underwriters (C.L.U.): membership of those who have earned the chartered life underwriter degree. Knowledge is centered on estate planning and life insurance.

American Society of Chartered Property and Casualty Underwriters (C.P.C.U.): membership of those who have passed all required examinations on property and casualty lines of insurance.

ancillary benefits: benefits for miscellaneous hospital charges.

annual renewable term: life insurance that may be renewed at the end of each year. The right to renew may extend to 10 or more years and the face value of the policy stays level, although the cost may increase with age.

annual statement: required annual report of an insurance company to the state insurance department showing assets, liabilities, receipts and disbursements, etc.

annuity: See Index.

annuity certain also known as **temporary annuity:** income for a specified period of time, with payment going to a beneficiary if the annuitant dies.

apportionment: proportionate method of dividing the

coverage (cost) when two or more companies cover the same loss.

appraisal: written opinion of an item, with a description and dollar value, by an impartial expert.

APS: abbr. of Attending Physician's Statement; the form filled out by doctors who have treated the proposed insured so that the insurance agent can prepare life, disability, or health insurance.

assigned risk: risk not acceptable to insurers and therefore assigned to insurers in a pool. Each participating company accepts its share of these risks.

assignment: life, property, or disability insurance assigned to another person; can be done in 2 ways: *collateral*, which means that the assignee has only the rights of the policy to protect his or her interest, and *absolute*, which means the assignee has all the same right as the original owner. The most common use is as collateral to protect mortgages on real property.

assurance: British word for insurance.

attractive nuisance: See Index.

authorization also known as **power of attorney** or **attorney in fact:** an insurance term giving written permission to 1) permit a company to inspect financial, medical, and moral records to determine eligibility for insurance, and 2) negotiate coverage rates to be charged on an insured's behalf.

average rate or **risk:** a single insurance note such as fire insurance for two or more business locations where inventory may flow back and forth.

beneficiary: the person to whom proceeds from an annuity or life insurance are payable. This term is carefully qualified in an insurance policy stating whether it is revocable, irrevocable, and whether there is a secondary beneficiary.

benefit: depending on conditions in an insurance contract, the money paid out to the recipient. There are many kinds of benefits in insurance parlance.

benefit period: the length of time benefits will be paid for any one accident, illness, or hospital stay.

Best's Reports: publication providing pertinent statistics, financial reports, and other information on all insurance companies doing business in the United States.

binder: a receipt given to a purchaser of insurance containing a new policy or new policyholder's terms which insures the policyholder until the actual policy is issued.

blanket insurance: insurance that covers more than one building, person, etc., in one policy.

broker: agent who represents the buyer of insurance and may buy policies from more than one company.

burning ratio: the ratio of losses suffered to the total insurance in effect.

cancellation: in insurance, the termination of a policy either by the policyholder or the insurance company before the end of its contract period.

carrier: an insurer or insurance company.

cash refund annuity: those installments still unpaid at the death of the annuitant paid to a designated beneficiary in one lump sum.

cash surrender value also known as **cashing in:** the monetary value of a life insurance policy when it is terminated by the policyholder during his or her lifetime.

cash value: the value of a whole life insurance policy against which one may borrow at a specific rate of interest stated in the contract.

casualty insurance: deals with insurance against loss due to legal liability to third person; has many subtitles such as auto, storekeeper, or fire when tenant is legally responsible.

catastrophe: severe and extreme loss such as of life or property; a special class of insurance. (See *Liability*.)

cede: to transfer to a reinsurer all or part of the insurance written by the relinquishing company because the cost is beyond the company's means. (See *reinsurance*.)

certificate of insurance: in group or individual insurance, a document stating the period one is insured, limitations, and coverage.

claim: following a loss, the request for reimbursement under an insurance contract as well as the final settlement.

clause: in an insurance policy, a section or paragraph that explains, defines, or clarifies the conditions of coverage.

co-insurance: a clause in health insurance under which the insured shares in losses to the extent of the percentages required by the insurance company at the time of the loss; the insurance company usually pays 80 percent and the policyholder 20 percent.

In property insurance the insured shares in the loss only if the policyholder does not insure at least to the percentage of value required by the insurance company. Therefore, if the loss is within or above the percentage required, the insured collects in full.

collision insurance: in automobile insurance, covers insured's own vehicle if it collides with another vehicle or object; does not cover bodily injury or property damage arising out of the collision.

Commissioners Standard Ordinary (CSO): a table of mortality approved by the National Association of Insurance Commissioners. This table is required as a minimum basis for use by all life insurance companies.

common disaster: in life insurance, the assumption of simultaneous death of the insured and beneficiary (as in a car accident) when there is no evidence of who died first.

completed operations insurance: liability insurance covering accidents after jobs have been completed. For example, a completed building may have a faulty elevator that does not cause trouble until a month after the contractor has finished the job. The insurance would cover bodily injury and/or property damage; this type of insurance would not pay for the elevator itself. Property insurance carried by the owner could cover the elevator.

composite rating: overall lowest rate of premium which takes into account more than one coverage of a business, such as automobile, general liability, and products liability.

comprehensive: that part of automobile insurance which includes insurance against theft, vandalism, or fire. Does not include collision or upset.

compulsory: required by law, such as automobile insurance.

concurrent insurance: two or more policies held by a property owner with the same conditions and coverages that cover the same interest in the same property.

conditional receipt: a term used when giving a receipt for a premium paid for a life and health insurance policy; coverage is effective from date of application and health examination provided insurability is established at the examination.

consequential loss coverage: insurance for a business interruption caused by a primary loss. For example, John Smith owns a music school. A fire damaged all the school's instruments, and classes had to be suspended. The instruments were the primary loss; the loss of tuition and time was a secondary loss.

constructive total loss: a loss great enough to make the repair as costly as or greater than the value of the property.

contractual or **assumed liability insurance:** a policy which covers a temporary user of a property for liability for which another is ordinarily responsible. Architects often require such a contract from a builder in order to transfer the liability for the construction away from themselves and to the builder.

contributory negligence also known as **comparative negligence:** a legal term used if an injured party fails to exercise proper care or contributes in other ways to negligence. The faulty action or lack of action will defeat the claim even though the other party is also negligent. Does not apply in all states.

conversion: the change from one policy to another.

convertible policy: term life insurance policy that can be changed to a whole life insurance policy.

corridor deductible: a health insurance term to denote a deductible amount between the benefits paid by the basic plan and the beginning of the major medical plan. A case in point is a major medical plan that goes into effect after the first $10,000 of costs. If the basic plan picks up only $8,000 of these initial costs, $2,000 will be the corridor deductible.

coverage also known as **protection:** the insurance policy's promise of payment in case of loss, liability, indemnity, etc.

death waiver: a clause in an insurance policy which states that certain causes of death will not be covered. Which specific causes are applicable depends on the individual policy.

declination: rejection of an application for insurance by an insurance company.

decreasing term insurance: life insurance of which the face value slowly decreases in scheduled steps from the time the policy becomes effective to the date the policy expires. The premiums remain constant. (See *term insurance*.)

deductible: Basic loss or expense the insurer must pay before an insurance policy pays benefits.

delay clause: provision in life insurance whereby the insurer may delay for a period of no longer than 6 months the granting of any loan against the cash value of the policy, except to pay the premiums on the policy.

DIC: abbr. of Difference in Conditions. A separate contract whenever property is involved that may need extremely broad coverage; coverage providing all risks of physical damage including earthquake and flood.

direct loss: damage which is a direct consequence of a particular peril. A fire in a car may cause a direct loss of the car.

direct-writing company: an insurance company that deals directly with its policyholders without intervention of independent agents or brokers.

disability: incapacity to work or function on the job or in private life. May be partial, total, temporary, or permanent.

disability waiver insurance: a rider available in life insurance providing that the insurance company will pay the premium if the policyholder is sick and disabled.

discovery period: the time allotted after the termination of an insurance policy or bond within which a loss or claim must be stated in order to be covered.

dividends: primarily in life insurance, the refund of a part of the premium after the company has set aside necessary reserves and made deductions for claims and expenses. There are many types of dividend insurance refunds, dividend deposits, accumulations, averaging, extras, options, etc.

donee beneficiary: a beneficiary who has never paid a premium. For example, a wife would be donee beneficiary when the husband pays for his own insurance policy and names his wife donee beneficiary. (See *beneficiary*.)

double indemnity: a clause in life insurance providing the beneficiary double the face value in case the policyholder dies from accidental means.

dread disease policy: health insurance providing a maximum of medical expenses arising out of diseases named in the policy such as cancer.

earned premium: the amount that has been used up during the term of an insurance policy after the fee of an insurance policy is paid. A policy which has been paid for a year, after 4 months would have a 4-month earned premium.

elimination period: the waiting period until benefits start in a health and disability policy.

encumbrance: See Index.

endorsement: the form used to make a change on any insurance policy such as replacing an old car with a new car.

endowment: a type of life insurance that promises to pay the face value to the beneficiary if the policyholder dies before the policy is completely paid for. If the policyholder is still living when the insurance policy is paid up, the full face value will be paid to the policyholder.

Equifax: a credit information company used by insurers to obtain information on applicants and claimants. Reports are known as Retail Credit Reports.

errors and omissions insurance also known as **malpractice**

insurance or **professional liability:** insurance against professional error or negligence which may cause loss and suffering.

estimated premium: estimated fee for insurance used mainly in large businesses where group insurance such as health insurance is involved; since the size of the group is variable and affects premium costs the true costs of premium will be known only at the end of the year.

In casualty insurance, including among others workers compensation, a final fee is determined by an audit by the insurance company at the end of the policy period.

examination: the auditing of an insurance company's books by the state for veracity.

exclusion: a peril of loss that is specifically excluded from coverage; flood, earthquake, war, nuclear reaction, etc.

expense ratio: the proportion of an insurance company's expenses to premiums.

experience: within a given time the record of claims made to and paid out by an insurance company. Determines premiums.

extended benefit: additional agreement broadening an insurance contract.

extended term: a nonforfeiture value; the cash value of a whole life insurance policy to purchase term insurance for the face value of the original policy. (See *nonforfeiture value.*)

face amount also known as **face value:** in life insurance, the full amount to be paid eventually upon the death of the insured.

facility of payment: a clause found in life insurance stating that under certain conditions, person(s) other than the beneficiary may receive payment.

Fair Credit Reporting Act: Public Law 91-508. If a client's request for insurance is declined because of poor credit rating, the applicant should be given the name of the reporting agency. The client may request a copy of the report and require an amendment of any errors in the report.

financed insurance: payment of life insurance premiums from money borrowed from the cash value of the policy.

financial responsibility law: a state law varying in degree from state to state which in essence requires insurance or other proof of the ability to pay for losses.

flat: without service or interest charges.

floater: a term referring to a policy covering movable property as long as it is within the territorial limits set in the contract. For example, a floater may be used to insure a precious fur coat.

fragmentation: a term used when several insurance companies share a larger risk by each taking a part of the coverage.

friendly fire: a fire in its right and proper place such as in a fireplace, barbecue, etc.

GL: abbr. of general liability; insurance maintained by businesses against bodily injury, property damage, and other operational hazards.

grace period: an extension of the due date for insurance premiums.

graded commission: an agent's fee that depends on class, type, or volume of insurance written.

grading schedule for cities and towns: rating by National Board of Fire Underwriters of areas such as cities and towns based on fire protection and water supply.

gross premium: net premium plus fees and other expenses.

grossline: the total limit on a specified risk or "class of business" such as a bowling alley, motel, or hotel that an insurance company is willing to accept.

group insurance: insurance bought by a group in order to benefit from lower premiums. The group may be under the umbrella of a place of employment, church, or other organization.

graduated life table: mortality possibilities calculated geographically and by formula.

guaranteed funds: provision of the Insurance Guarantee

Act that insurance companies pool funds to pay unpaid claims or to bail out a company near bankruptcy.

guaranteed renewable: usually in health insurance, the right of the insured to continue his insurance for a substantial time by paying his premiums and not making any changes in the policy while the contract is in force. A premium rate change can be permissible.

hazard also known as **morale hazard:** anything that may increase the possibility of loss, harm, liability, or infraction on health such as a leaking roof, unsanitary conditions in an institution, etc.

HIAA: abbr. of Health Insurance Association of America; Life and Health insurers provide research and education and are active in Washington, D.C., all for the promotion of voluntary private health insurance. HII (Health Insurance Institute) is the branch of HIAA that concerns itself mostly with the outflow of information.

HMO: abbr. of Health Maintenance Organization; Members pay a premium for which the individual or the family receives complete health care from internists and specialists.

hold harmless agreement: See *contractual liability insurance*.

homeowner's policy: provides protection against liability and other losses such as theft, fire, etc., to which a homeowner or renter is exposed.

hull insurance: special insurance for yachts, speedboats, houseboats, or cargo ships.

human life value: estimate of the earning power of an individual from present age to retirement.

"if" clause: a clause terminating coverage when certain conditions are discovered, such as misrepresentation, fire hazards, etc.

IIA (Insurance Institute of America, Inc.): organization that develops recognized programs and gives national examinations and diplomas in most facets of insurance.

III (Insurance Information Institute): organization that deals with public relations programs of various segments of property and liability insurance.

IIS (International Insurance Seminars, Inc.): an organization of insurance people noted primarily for its annual seminars which allows academicians as well as insurance practitioners to exchange ideas.

in kind: the right of the insurer to replace the loss with the equivalent material or object rather than with cash.

increased cost of construction: rise in replacement cost that may cause the price to be higher than the original building cost.

indemnify: to make good a loss.

indemnity: the repair, payment, or replacement of a loss.

inherent vice: a fault that leads to inevitable destruction and therefore not covered by the insurance.

insolvency clause also known as **strike through:** stipulation that the reinsurer must pay his share of a loss even though the primary insurer has become insolvent. In bankruptcy cases the amount is paid directly to the insured and not the liquidator.

inspection: examination usually by an independent company to check the facts about an applicant.

insurable risk: applicant that meets the standards of the insurance company; the insurer is able to calculate the chance of loss.

insurance: a pooling of money to share an individual's losses, catastrophies, accidents and health problems; not for the profit of the individual policyholder. Costs are figured on the basis of statistics.

insurance carrier: the insurer.

insurance commissioner: the head of the state's insurance regulatory agency.

insurance policy: the contract between the insurer and the insured.

insurance services office: rate-setting body for all lines of property and casualty insurance.

insuring agreement: the heart of a policy; states the period of the contract perils, and names the who, what, when and how of the insurance coverage.

joint insurance: life insurance written on two or more persons with benefits payable usually at the first death.

judgment rates also known as **A rates:** rates based on the underwriter's judgment rather than by loss experience. (See *experience*.)

key person insurance: life or disability insurance bought by a company or employer to cover a person who contributes substantially to the success of the business.

lapsed policy: a policy that has expired because of nonpayment of premiums.

last clear chance: a term for the doctrine that one who had the very last chance to avoid an accident is liable.

law of large numbers also known as **degree of risk, odds** and **probability:** examination of statistics during a given period and of a large number of people to calculate the ratio of loss, risk, and deaths.

ledger cost: the net cost of life insurance. The company subtracts the present cash value of the policy less the premiums paid and less all dividends.

level premium insurance: life insurance for which the premium remains the same throughout the contract. Since payments are usually less in the beginning and more in the later years, the "level" is usually the average.

level term insurance: term policy the face value of which remains the same from the effective date until expiration date. (See *term*.)

liability: money to be paid out; money owed; obligations, anticipated obligations and losses.

liability insurance: coverage against loss, unexpected damage or obligations, and responsibility to others. An automobile driver has an obligation of safety to other drivers and pedestrians as well as property.

liability limits: the maximum amount the insurance contract will pay in case of responsible obligation.

life insurance: risk sharing under which the insured gives contributions which the insurer reinvests to pay out to a beneficiary when the insured dies. There are various types of life insurance among which are *whole life* and *endowment*.

line sheet: a guide outlining the limits of liability to be assumed by the insurance for different classes of risks.

loading: the added costs of operating an insurance and the risk that losses will be greater than statistically expected. The opposite of "pure" insurance, which is only the estimated cost necessary for losses.

loan value: the amount of money that may be borrowed from the cash value of an insurance policy.

loss: 1) an insured's claim; the amount paid out by an

insurance company to cover a claim; 2) the reduction of the value of a piece of property because of a peril making it difficult or expensive to insure.

loss of use insurance: coverage against inability to use whatever is insured (such as a store or a vehicle) because of damage or loss.

loss payable: in case of loss, payment provided to someone other than a policyholder. For example, a car bought with a loan would need a policy to protect the lending institution.

loss ratio: the proportion of losses to premiums.

loss reserve: estimated liability for losses due but not yet paid.

losses incurred: total losses in a given period.

major medical: medical insurance with large deductibles that takes over where basic insurance leaves off. Covers "catastrophic" medical expenses in and out of the hospital.

malicious mischief: See *V&MM*.

malinger: feign disability to collect longer than necessary disability insurance.

malpractice insurance: coverage that protects professionals such as doctors and lawyers against claims of poor judgment and pays damages set by the court.

mass merchandising: method of selling insurance to a group of people or businesses with common requirements; the group mails in the premium in one lump sum to one company and for one master contract.

master-servant rule: a legal term stating that employers are obligated to protect the public from employees' acts.

maturity: when a life insurance policy's face value becomes payable.

mental distress: condition leading to a claim which is usually honored if the claimant was physically involved but not if the claimant was a bystander. Exceptions have been made in a few extreme cases.

merit rating: an individual's loss record upon which premiums depend; most commonly used in automobile insurance.

minimum rate: low premiums because risk factor is low.

misstatement of age: a uniform provision for individual life insurance policy as to what action is to be taken in misinformation about age.

morbidity rate: statistics in given diseases, disorders, related age groups, and groups in general in comparison to well persons, all within a given time.

mortgage insurance: a policy promising to pay in case of death a mortgagor's mortgage completely or to continue installment payments.

Mutual Benefit Association: organization to which no fixed premiums are paid but members are levied costs of losses as they occur.

Mutual Insurance Company: company of which each policyholder is a member. Dividends may or may not be paid to the policyholders.

negligence: failure of care by action and/or omission; lack of reasonable prudence. There are in legal terminology many types of negligence: gross (willful), comparative (proportionally), contributory and presumed.

no-fault insurance: type of automobile insurance that stipulates that no matter whose fault an automobile accident is, the victim can collect damages and medical expenses directly from his or her insurance; practiced by most states, but not by all, and there are major variations from state to state.

noncancelable: the same as *guaranteed renewable*, except that the premium must remain as stated in the policy at the time of issue.

nonforfeiture value: the value of a life policy when it is terminated by other than death. The value is expressed either in cash, extended term, or reduced paid-up insurance.

noninsurable risk: a risk possibility so high that insurance cannot be written on it; a risk possibility that cannot be measured.

nonownership automobile liability: protection against liability when someone other than the insured drives the car in question.

omnibus clause: clause that extends coverage to include persons other than the policyholder.

other insurance clause: statement of what is to be done in case a hazard, liability, or claim is covered by more than one policy.

overinsured: the condition in which an individual has purchased more insurance than needed to replace a loss so that it becomes profitable for the insured to have a loss and to make a claim. In some states loss recovery is limited to actual loss sustained regardless of how much insurance was originally purchased.

package insurance: one policy including several coverages that would ordinarily be in separate policies.

PAR: abbr. of participating. An insurance company that distributes dividends (when declared) to its policyholders.

partnership insurance: mutual insurance of partners in a business, each partner insuring the other. If one dies, the other can then afford to buy the decedent's partnership in the business from the heirs.

Paul versus Virginia: a landmark case in 1869. The Supreme Court decided that insurance is a business and not commerce and therefore should be regulated by each state and not by the federal government.

peril: the cause of a possible loss.

permanent disability: usually defined as the inability of the insured to perform his or her usual and regular occupation.

physical hazard: See *hazard*.

policy: the complete insurance contract including the name of the insurer, insured, riders, clauses and endorsements.

policy dividend: in some types of insurance the return of part of the fee; usually the difference between gross premium charged and the actual costs as calculated according to the company's actuarial formula.

policy loan: a loan made by the insurance company to the owner of a life insurance policy using the life insurance's cash value as security.

pool: a method of *reinsurance*. Often a group of insurance companies will form a group and proportion the risk and premiums among themselves so that the cost of the loss is not too great for any one company. Automobile drivers with high liability records are placed in a pool insurance. Commercial aircrafts because of their need for high coverage are in a pool insurance.

portfolio reinsurance: the assumption of the reinsurer of all or part of the ceding insurer's business in one or all categories. (See *reinsurance* and *cede*.)

portfolio return: resumption by a ceding company of a portfolio formerly reinsured.

preferred risk: a risk deemed less risky than the average on which it was calculated.

preliminary term: insurance issued to cover risk up to a certain date at which time the policyholder may wish to renew, always paying premiums on this particular date.

premium: the fee of specified insurance protection for a specified period.

present value: present worth of premiums which, if invested at certain interest rates, will at a future date have an increased value. The present value of the money is less than at some future date. This is used primarily in life insurance calculations where premiums may be paid on a monthly basis.

presumed negligence also known as **res ipsa loquitur:** a legal term meaning "the facts speak for themselves." An injury or damage occurred because of the negligence of the one responsible; for example, the owner of a house who has an exceedingly slippery waxed kitchen floor may cause someone to fall.

primary coverage: the amount covered after the deductible; coverage from the first dollar.

primary insurer: in *reinsurance*, the one who originated the business and ceded it.

principal sum: claim or benefits paid in one sum, especially when a contract provides benefits for accidental death or dismemberment.

prior approval rating forms: the term used to show that rate changes must be approved by the state insurance department before the company can use them.

private mortgage insurance: See Index.

probability: the chances of an event occurring expressed in a formula between 0 and 10, and calculated on a fraction basis.

producer: one who sells insurance; an agent or solicitor.

prohibited list: a list of types of risks an insurance company will not insure.

protected risk: a piece of property within the area of a fire department.

protection: coverage under the terms in an insurance policy.

public adjuster: a licensed person who represents the insured for a fee in a loss; assumes duties of the insured making an inventory of the losses, getting estimates for repairs and negotiating a settlement with the insurance company.

pure loss cost: a ratio used by insurance companies for a given period to figure out their losses of reinsurance plus allocated loss expenses compared to gross earned premiums.

pure premium: that part of the net fee needed to pay expected losses; used to determine insurance rates.

pure risk: a 50–50 chance as to whether there will be a loss or gain.

rate: the cost of insurance figured per unit. For example, in property insurance one insures per $100 of value. The *premium* is the rate times the number of units of insurance purchased. Thus if a piece of property costs $1,000, and it costs $1 per $100 of value to insure, one would multiply 10 $100 units times $1. The premium would be $10.

rating bureau: a private organization which concerns itself with data on hazards, risks, rates in various geographic areas, and the compilation and measurements of such data necessary to insurance companies.

rating class: the degree and category a risk is considered.

recapture: the taking back by a ceding company (see *cede*) of the insurance it ceded.

reciprocal insurance exchange: an incorporated group of individuals who mutually insure each other, each assuming a portion of risk.

reimbursement: payment of a loss covered by the policy.

reinsurance: the spreading of a risk too large for one insurer by sharing the risk as well as a portion of the premium with another company.

reinsurance broker: an individual or organization who seeks out reinsurance for ceding companies. (See *cede* and *reinsurance*.)

renewal certificate: official statement used to renew a policy and uphold all the provisions in the original document; keeps the original document valid.

rider: a waiver, an endorsement, a paragraph, or a clause attached to a policy. It may be to delete, expand, or add a coverage.

risk: uncertainty of an outcome when a chance of loss exists; coverage of a person or thing.

safe driver plan: a form of merit rating for automobile drivers; each violation and certain traffic accidents are given points which in turn affect drivers' automobile insurance premiums.

salvage: property taken over by an insurer to reduce loss.

settlement: claim payment after the insured and insurer have agreed on the amount.

shock loss: a loss so great that it affects the insurer's rates.

short rate premium: premium for less than a year (Most premiums are for one year). If the insured cancels after 6 months, his rate will be higher than 50 percent of one year.

standard policy: identical insurance regardless of which insurance company issues the policy; insurance in compliance with state law; insurance issued to a standard risk (See *standard risk.*)

standard risk: a person entitled to insurance without extra rating or special restrictions. A term especially used in health and life insurance.

state fund: those funds set up by the state government to finance mandatory insurance. Varies from state to state in that it may be monopolistic or competitive.

statutory reserve: as required by law the reserve needed by every insurer.

stop loss: 1) a provision to limit losses to protect the insurer from suffering too great a loss. 2) a *reinsurance* term whereby the reinsurer takes over only after the ceding (see *cede*) company has incurred losses which exceed a specified loss ratio.

subrogation clause: right of the insurer to pursue any course of action in the company's or the insured's name against a third party who is liable for a claim which has been paid by the policyholder's company.

surrender: a term used in life insurance when the insured terminates his or her life insurance and is given the cash value of the policy.

term: the period of time for which a policy is issued.

term insurance: an agreement between the insured and an insurance company whereby the insurance company promises to pay the face amount of the policy if the insured dies within a specified time period. If the insured survives the period, the contract expires without value. There are many varieties of term insurance. (See *convertible policy*.)

Many young people like term insurance because it is less expensive than other types of life insurance. Jane and Tom, for example, got married when they were both 20 years old. When they were expecting their first child they decided, even though Tom was in excellent health, that it would be wise to have a five-year term insurance policy, because they did not have any assets or savings. If something happened to Tom, Jane and the baby would have some instant assets.

time limit: the allotted period within which notice of claim and proof of loss must be submitted to an insurance company.

title insurance: See Index.

tort insurance: liability insurance against a wrong committed against an individual. The wrong may be independent of a contract and may be considered a private wrong.

traumatic injury: physical damage to one's body caused accidentally and not from disease or illness.

tsunami damage: special insurance for buildings in a flood area or in a tidal-wave zone in order for them to be eligible for a mortgage.

underwriter: 1) The one who signs his name on the insurance contract. An insurance company itself may be the underwriter. 2) the expert who selects the risks the insurance company can accept and up to what amount and on what terms the risks can be accepted.

unearned premium: on an insurance balance sheet, those fees paid in but not yet used up on the calendar of time. For example, for car insurance paid in advance every 6 months, there would be 5 months of unearned premium after the first month has passed.

unemployment insurance: insurance against loss of income due to unemployment. Unemployment insurance is funded by payroll taxes and subject to control by both federal and state governments.

unilateral contract: an agreement in which only one party makes promises. Most insurance policies are unilateral because the insurer makes all the promises while the insured keeps the policy in force by paying the premiums.

uninsured motorists coverage: clause found in most automobile insurance. The insurance company will pay damages for bodily injuries when their client is hit by a hit-and-run driver or by an uninsured driver. A minority of states have property damage coverage automatically included.

valuation: the appraisal of items to be insured such as jewelry, silverware, fur coats, etc.

valued policy: the statement by the policy that a determined amount will be paid in the event of a total loss.

V&MM: abbr. of Vandalism and Malicious Mischief; willful damage and destruction to property excluding theft.

vesting rights: upon termination of employment, the right to the employee's share of the money in a pension plan funded by the employer.

voidable: renderable of no legal effect by either party to a contract. The insured may void a policy by not paying his premiums, and the insurer may cancel if the insured commits certain acts.

waiver: a clause excluding liability; a clause excluding a known right; for example, the insurance company may give up its rights to collect premiums during a period of disability of the insured.

whole life insurance: insurance the face value of which is only paid upon the death of the insured; has cash value and in some cases may pay dividends.

will ride: coverage for loss regardless of the geographical location.

workers' compensation: a law requiring that the employer provide insurance that will pay benefits to an employee or his or her beneficiary if the employee is injured or suffers death or disability as a result of occupational hazard.

FINANCIAL STATEMENTS

accelerated depreciation: a formula which allocates the cost of an asset over its useful life so that more of the cost is deducted from income in earlier years than in later years.

accounting: recording and summarizing an individual's or business's financial position and activities.

accounts and **notes receivable:** amounts owed to a company and therefore representing cash that should be coming into the company; for example, Y's Department Store had 2,000 charge customers. On December 31, when Y's closed its books for the year, its charge customers cumulatively owed the store $1 million. The store knew that it would be receiving $1 million from the collection of its accounts.

accounts payable: to whom and how much a business, individual, company or corporation owes money; it may be for raw material, services and other needs. In a general ledger, accounts payable are recorded as one total sum (after individual postings).

accumulated depreciation: the cost of the asset which has been assigned to the expenses of the company since the asset has been acquired. Yearly expense is calculated by dividing the original cost by its estimated lifetime. If a piece of equipment depreciates $50 each year, after 3 years the accumulated depreciation would be $150.

additional paid-in capital: additional monies or properties received from sale of capital stock above par value.

adjusted trial balance: the original balance updated by new entries.

administrative expenses: general expenses of a business as contrasted to expenses incurred by specific functions of the enterprise, such as selling expenses and financing costs.

allowance method: monetary need as estimated from past experiences. For example, if every year a certain percentage of customers don't pay their bills, an allowance can be calculated and deducted from accounts receivable.

amortization: the cost of an intangible asset (a patent, goodwill, trademark) spread out over the life of the asset; as the expense is shown on income statement, the value of the asset decreases. (Not to be confused with the amortization of a bond or mortgage.)

annual report: the formal statement issued yearly by a company for its stockholders, among others, showing assets, liabilities, earnings and other information of interest.

assets: anything owned by an individual or a business; includes cash, investments, receivables, inventories as well as fixed and intangible assets.

audit: examination of accounting records by an independent accounting firm to determine whether the financial statements are prepared in conformity with generally accepted accounting principles.

balance sheet: a summary of the assets, liabilities, and capital of a person or enterprise.

bank reconciliation: a means of explaining the difference between the bank balance on the bank statement versus the balance of cash in the ledger. For example, the difference may be due to an uncleared check.

book value: the sum of the assets less the sum of the liabilities of a company. Sometimes a company is worth more than the book value shows because such items as building, equipment, etc., are always presented at their depreciated values. Furthermore, a company's general reputation, trademark and track record, which are all intangibles and which contribute to a company's value, are usually unrecorded.

book value per share: the sum of the assets less the sum of the liabilities and preferred stockholders' equity of a company, divided by the number of common shares outstanding.

business segment reporting: requirement that those companies involved in 2 or more lines of business report sales and contributions to earnings by their business segments or product lines. For example, XYZ Company manufactures 10 different items. Only 2 items sell well. It is of interest to stockholders to have a detailed report of each one of the 10 lines. Otherwise, the stockholders won't know which line contributed the most to the company's profitability and if management is paying too much attention to the losers.

capital: funds invested in the business by stockholders; includes stocks, reinvested earnings, and preferred stock.

capital expenditure: a major addition to a business, such as buildings, equipment, tools, vehicles.

capital statement: statement of owner's rights to assets in a business. The usual calculation is to take the owner's investment at the beginning of the year plus the company's profits and subtract the owner's withdrawals. The result is the most recent owner equity.

capital structure: relation of long-term debts to preferred and common stock, additional paid-in capital, and retained earnings.

capitalization ratio: the percentages of the total investments in a company by type—common stock, preferred stock and long-term debt. The higher the ratio of common stock equity, the less prior claims on the company are ahead of the common stockholders.

cash disbursement journal: record of the outflow of money in cash or bank checks that shows in which account the payment ultimately was posted.

cash flow: the difference between cash receipts and cash disbursements. Inflows of cash result from profitable operations, issuance of long-term debt, and sale of capital stock. Outflows are cash from unprofitable operations, acquisition of fixed assets, reduction of long-term debts, and reduction in capital, including dividends to shareholders. In essence, the cash flow shows from where money comes in, and for what it is spent by the business.

cash receipts journal: a book recording incoming money.

changes in components of working capital: a statement presented by a corporation showing the effect of its financing and investing activities in its current assets and liabilities. It includes increases and decreases in current assets such as cash, marketable securities, accounts receivable, and inventories. Also shown are increases and decreases in current liabilities such as accounts payable, accrued liabilities, current maturity of long-term debt, dividends payable, and income and other taxes.

chart of accounts: declaration of account titles being used and their corresponding classified listing. For example, assets might have 5 subheadings (cash, accounts receivable, land, building and office equipment). Office equipment might be classified as number 30.

classified balance sheet: a highly detailed statement breaking down assets and liabilities to specific headings such as current and long-term.

combined or **overall coverage:** result of dividing annual interest bond holders and debt costs into operating profit (before taxes have been paid). If Company X earned $1,000 before taxes, and owed $500 interest to debt holders, Company X could afford to pay the interest twice; thus, the overall coverage is 2.

consolidated balance sheet: a balance sheet showing the financial condition of a corporation and its subsidiaries.

controlling accounts: a summary account with totals equal to entries and balances appearing in individual accounts in a subsidiary ledger.

cost of goods sold: the cost to produce or acquire a product; this may include raw material, wages, electricity and other costs.

CPA (Certified Public Accountant): accountant who has passed all parts of a state exam qualifying him or her for a license to practice accounting.

current assets: those assets a company expects to receive, turn into cash or use up within a year or less; included may be cash, accounts receivable, inventories, prepaid rent and supplies.

current liability: the money presently owed and due by a company within the next twelve months.

current maturity of long-term debt: the amount due in the next year; some debts may require partial annual repayment over a period of years.

current ratio also known as **working capital ratio:** figure used by financial analysts to measure sufficient levels of working capital. For instance:

$$\frac{\$400 \text{ current assets}}{\$200 \text{ current liabilities}} = \$2.$$

For each $2 of current assets, there is $1 of current liabilities.

deferral: for business purposes, postponement of the recognition of a sale or an expense until the money is used up, or postponement of the recognition of an expense until the merchandise is used up. For example, a monthly magazine may receive money for a 1-year subscription, but may post the income as unearned revenue until it delivers the 12 issues.

deficit: condition of a company whose retained earnings show a debit balance due to operational losses.

definite liabilities: monetary amount which is certain such as bonds, notes, interests, accounts due, salaries.

departmental margin: each department's contribution to the company's complete operation. The contribution is calculated as follows:

Income − Cost of Goods = Gross Profit
Gross Profit − Direct Expenses = Contribution

depletion accounting: an accounting practice in bookkeeping where charges are made against earnings made from the use of natural resources. The accounting allows for the fact that the natural resource in question may eventually be used up. These resources include oil, gas, timber, coal, and metals.

depreciation: original cost allocated to expense over the estimated life of the asset. (See *accumulated depreciation.*)

dividend payout: the percentage of earnings on the common stock that is paid out in dividends. Some companies keep a part of the earnings in order to expand the company or to have an extra cash flow.

dividend return: yearly income one receives from a stock. John Smith owns 100 shares of XYZ stock which he bought at $25 a share at a total value of $2,500. His dividend is $200 a year: 8 percent of his total investment or $2 per share.

dividends payable: preferred or common stock dividends or both declared by the board of directors but not yet paid. Because they have been declared, it is an obligation and a liability.

double-entry bookkeeping: system of accounting in which each entry is recorded twice, once on the debit side and once on the credit side.

earnings before income tax: operating profit minus interest owed to stockholders and other debt holders.

ending inventory: the amount of material or goods available at the end of a fiscal period.

equity: the claims of the stockholders against the assets of the company.

estimated liabilities: predictable liabilities such as income tax and employees' pensions.

expenses: in bookkeeping terminology, any costs involving the running of the company. Expenses may be broken down into categories and units such as sales, production, research and administration.

FIFO (first-in, first-out): an inventory costing or valuation method which assumes that inventory bought first will be sold first. For example, Jane Smith, who owns a gourmet food store, ordered the same brand of jam twice. The first order of 12 jars cost $12. The second order, even though it was the same size and quantity, cost $14. At the end of the year she had 6 jars left. Her accountant marked the 12 jars for $12 sold, and used the FIFO principal to mark the 6 jars left at higher price of $7. (See *LIFO*.)

fiscal year: a regular period of time in which a company does its accounting before starting a new 12-month accounting period. Not all companies are able to use the calendar year. For example, department stores which do most of their business at Christmastime find it difficult to end their year on December 31.

fixed assets: assets with a life in excess of one year; may include buildings, land, machinery, equipment, and motor vehicles.

fixed charges: fixed expenses are costs that do not vary with volume of activity.

freight in: an account entry showing transportation expenses of inventory.

fund statement: a statement that shows the financing and investing activities and changes in working capital from one balance sheet to the next.

funded debt: debts secured by committing specific assets to a sinking fund.

funds: net working capital available.

general journal: record of miscellaneous transactions.

general ledger: the principal ledger containing income statements and balance sheets.

going concern: a business doing so well according to the accounting ledgers that it will not go out of business within the foreseeable future.

gross profit: direct profit. Only the direct cost of the goods (such as raw material and labor) is subtracted from the sale of the goods.

gross sales: measure of goods sold before deductions, returns, price allowances and discounts.

horizontal analysis: a method of comparing statements by showing the rate and amount of change across columns of statements from period to period.

index: a means of measuring against and comparing to a base year (sample year) by percentages.

intangible assets: assets that do not have a physical presence but contribute to the company's future and growth. Goodwill, franchises, trademarks, patents and copyrights are all intangible assets.

interest coverage ratio: figure arrived at by dividing operating profit by annual interest charges.

interest expenses: interest paid or due on debts and listed as liabilities to a company.

inventory: raw materials, work in process as well as finished products measured at cost or market value—whichever is lower—and listed as an asset on the balance sheet.

inventory turnover ratio: figure calculated by dividing the cost of goods sold in the most recent year by the average of the inventory of the last 12 months. For example, Jan's dress shop sold $12,000 worth of blouses within the past year; the average number of blouses in the inventory within the last 12 months was 600; the turnover ratio of a blouse was

$$\frac{\$12{,}000}{600} \text{ or a cost of 5 to 1.}$$

liabilities: all claims against a business or person such as unpaid bills, taxes, rent, wages, loans, debts, promissory notes, and interest dues.

liability contingencies: liabilities whose payment depends on the outcome of a future event; may include goods sold under warranty, court outcome of product defects or new tax assessment.

LIFO (last-in, first-out): an inventory costing or valuation method which assumes that inventory bought most recently is sold first. For example, Carol Dean, who owns a blouse boutique, features Mr. Y designer blouses. She placed 2 separate orders for 12 blouses each, each order for the same style, to be delivered 2 weeks apart. The first order cost $120 per dozen and the second order cost $140 per dozen. When her accountant did the end-of-the-month inventory, he used the LIFO method because he assumed the newest item would sell the fastest. (See *FIFO.*)

liquidity ratio: a measure of how quickly a company can raise or provide cash. The ratio is derived by subtracting inventories from current assets and dividing by the current liabilities:

$$\frac{\text{current assets} - \text{inventories}}{\text{current liabilities}}$$

long-term liabilities also known as **long-term debts** or **fixed liabilities:** in a business any services, obligations, mortgages, bonds and other debts that are not due for a year or more.

marketable securities: securities carried in the balance sheet and computed at cost or current market value—whichever is less.

minimum legal capital: the amount a corporation is required to keep in the business for the protection of the creditors. Usually it is the par value of the total issued stocks. Each state has its own regulations.

net asset value per share: figure used by investment companies to compute their company's worth by totaling the market value of all securities owned. All liabilities are deducted and the balance divided by the number of shares outstanding.

net income for the year: term for earnings or profits after all costs have been deducted. More commonly called "the bottom line."

net loss: the amount arrived at when expenses are greater than profit.

net pay: wages minus all deductions such as social security, taxes, etc.

net sales: total cash earned in a business minus discounts, sales returns and other allowances.

operating profit: figure arrived at by deducting costs of goods, selling and administrative expenses and depreciation from sales; taxes and interest charges are not deducted.

operating profit margin: profit calculated as a percentage of sales before deducting depreciation, interest and taxes; this margin is considered a basic indicator of efficiency of operations.

operations: breakdown of sales, earnings, costs, and expenses.

paid-in capital: amount originally invested in the business by the stockholders at par value of the shares. Paid-in capital is listed on the balance sheet as a segment of stockholders' equity.

par: the dollar amount of a company's common shares on the balance sheet.

posting: placement of a transaction into a ledger from a journal. Both the ledger and journal show the page number from which the information came or to which it was transferred.

purchase discount account: account showing a credit or savings because a bill or bills were paid early. For example, Joe's Department Store bought 150 pairs of men's boots for $3,000. The terms of the sale were that the purchaser would receive 5 percent off the bill if paid before the end of the month. Since Joe paid before the end of the month, he entered the bill as follows in his account book:

	Debit	Credit
Accounts payable	$ 3,000	
Purchase discount		$ 150
Cash		2,850

quarterly data: presentation of sales and earnings results on a three-month basis.

receivables: bills owed to the company and placed in the assets column of the ledger.

residual value also known as **salvage value:** the resale or scrap value of a piece of equipment when it has reached the end of its usefulness to the company. This estimation is subtracted from the cost of the equipment to arrive at the amount of depreciation.

retained earnings: accumulated earnings reinvested in the business. Essentially, it is a summation of annual earnings minus dividends and other charges.

sales-to-fixed-asset ratio: a financial relationship determined by dividing annual sales by the value of property, plant and equipment. The ratio shows if funds are productively invested.

statement of income: statement showing sales less cost, expenses, taxes, interest and depreciation.

straight-line method of depreciation: a formula used to calculate the total amount of depreciation allowed to a company's assets (machines, vehicles, plant) over their estimated life. One takes the original cost of the equipment minus salvage value and divides by the number of years to be depreciated. For example, if Company X buys a car for $8,000 to be used for 4 years and which, after 4 years, can still be sold for $4,000, the annual depreciation according to this formula is $1,000.

total current assets: at the present moment, available cash, marketable securities, accounts and notes receivable, and current inventories as cited on the company's balance sheet.

voucher system: an internal control system used in large companies by which any expense or purchase is recorded for each check drawn.

work sheet: a rough draft in which an accountant summarizes the data needed to complete a final statement.

INVESTING – IN A SMALL BUSINESS

advertisement: the means by which the public is made aware of a product; includes 1) choice of medium (newspaper, television, radio, magazine, billboard, or direct mail), 2) cost effective rate (amount of business to be generated from the investment), and 3) figuring out the required investment level, the amount in dollars required to produce an effective business campaign in the chosen medium.

authority: the ultimate responsibility borne by the owner(s) in all decision-making.

average: a number typical of a group of numbers, such as the average wage, or average sale.

average markup: the practice of using the same percentage markup for each item when a business carries many items.

balance of trade: the national difference in money value of national imports and exports.

bankruptcy: declaration of insolvency, after which financial affairs are administered by the court through a receiver or trustee; may be 1) voluntary: applied for and granted by the court, or 2) involuntary: petitioned for by creditors and granted by the court.

BEAM: abbr. of Bidders Early Alert Message; an arm of the National Small Business Association, a nationwide data network geared to disseminating government contractual information.

brand: a name, term, symbol, sign, and/or design used to identify the product of a firm.

break-even volume: the basic amount of sales needed to pay for keeping a business running without loss or profit. Total fixed costs divided by selling price minus variable cost per unit equals the basic break-even point.

broker also known as **merchandise agent:** agent without title to merchandise he or she sells who receives income from commissions and fees.

Bureau of the Census: agency that reports vital and valuable statistics on demographics throughout the nation with some studies of special interest to businesses.

business liquidation auction: sale at which equipment from heavy machinery to office equipment—all valuable assets—is auctioned to the highest bidder.

call: service available through the Small Business Administration that provides management consultants to economically and socially disadvantaged small businesses.

charting revenues: keeping track of income from units sold. If a manufacturer has to sell 300 units in order to cover all his costs, it is important for the company to keep track of its income.

collection agency: a firm engaged in collecting overdue accounts for others.

Commerce Business Daily: a U.S. Department of Commerce publication (U.S. Commerce Department, Washington, DC 20233); publishes a list of "qualified products" and notices of intent to establish a new list or to expand the number of sources available; manufacturers listed can produce products according to set qualifications. (See *qualified products list*.)

conglomerate: an affiliation of companies in dissimilar lines of business. (See *conglomerate* in "Stock Market Trading Terms.")

consignment sales: products not paid for at the time of delivery to sales outlet; products to be paid for only when sold.

Consumer Price Index: the rise or fall of the cost of goods to the consumer as compared to a base year; a means of tracking inflation.

controlling: comparing actual results to planned results and taking corrective action.

cooperative: a group of small companies with similar products, services, or interests, banded together for economic advantages. The cooperators are shareholders in the cooperative. The most common are agricultural markets, real estate, groups and consumer cooperatives.

corporation: a separate legal entity entirely apart from its owner(s); may have sole ownership or may have stockholders. A corporation continues to function regardless of the death or departure of its stockholders; in most cases, creditors have claims only against the assets of the corporation. (See *legal personality*.)

correlation: the relationship between two or more variables.

delinquent accounts: accounts receivable overdue.

demography: study of population, including density, growth rates, occupational trends, income levels, birth and death rate and consumer behavior.

Department of Commerce: a branch of the federal government; assists in international and national trade, gives grants to help build public facilities essential to industrial and commercial development, makes available world and national trade data and educational materials; responsible for a wide range of regulation enforcement.

Department of Labor: federal department concerned with labor–management affairs, regulations, mediation, and labor law enforcement as well as education.

director: a manager of a corporation, bank or other business institution. Federal and state laws prescribe as to who may and may not be elected director to certain types of business institutions. See directors in "Stock Market Trading Terms."

discount: reduction in price. There are various types of discounts:

1) trade discounts—the reduced price offered by the manufacturer to the retailer;
2) quantity discounts—the reduction of price in relation to the size of the purchase;
3) cumulative quantity discounts—the totaling of consecutive orders to qualify for a discount;
4) cash discounts—the percentage amount permitted off a bill when paid within 10 days;
5) seasonal discounts—the reduced price of seasonal items such as skis or air conditioners when bought off-season.

employee incentive plan: awards in the form of either extra pay, or pay by the amount produced rather than by the hour, or prizes such as paid vacation for better-than-average production.

entrepreneur: someone with capital—or who knows how to raise capital—who conceives and develops business(es); someone who takes risks and responsibility, and expects to take profits from the business he or she conceives.

exchange control: the act of limiting or banning the flow of local currency into dollars.

Federal Trade Commission: an independent federal agency acting as a trade regulatory body; responsible for laws assuring free and fair competition, interpreting antitrust laws and laws protecting the consumer against deceptive practices.

fictitious name statement: a legal record of who actually owns a business if a business is run under a fictitious name.

financial analyst: expert who interprets data, statistics, yields, costs and future trends in order to increase business.

FOB: a term meaning "free on board." Items to be delivered to the specified designation are transported free up to the time they are placed on a public carrier.

foreign correspondent: a bank in a foreign country acting for, and maintaining money for, a domestic bank.

foreign exchange rate: the number of foreign currency exchange units for each dollar.

franchise: company that may represent and sell a product or services of a parent company in a specific territory; may also be a distribution or producing concern. Depending on the contract, the parent company profits by either outright payment, a share of the receipts, and/or agreement by the franchise to buy supplies or equipment from the parent organization.

fringe benefits: financial advantages and supplementary rewards other than salaries such as insurance and pension plans.

general partner(s): the same as *proprietor*, except that more than one person is pooling efforts. A contract declares rights and responsibility in the operation of the firm.

graph: a chart, diagram, or picture showing the relationships of data to each other.

gross national product (GNP): national market value comprised of national income (total earnings of labor and property) plus product accounts (national production of all goods and services produced in a year); a national total of consumer purchases, government purchases, gross private domestic investments, and export of goods and services; helps to chart the national economic trend including prosperity, recession, and depression, and to estimate changes in the standard of living of the population.

holding company: a business which owns the securities of another—in most cases with voting rights.

image: the company as visualized by the target population; a message that management creates and may change at any time. For example, packaging helps to create a view of the company.

independent contractor: an individual who signs a form agreeing to perform certain duties on a contractual basis rather than as an employee.

index: See Index.

index number: in business, a percentage used to compare calculations and figures as costs or prices within a standard period.

industrial designer: an artist who takes an invention and houses it attractively; used by automobile manufacturers, washing-machine manufacturers, etc.

institutional advertising: advertising aimed at creating goodwill for a company. An example is an oil company's advertisement explaining how they protect wildlife while drilling for oil.

inventory: See *LIFO* and *FIFO*.

key person insurance: See Index.

labor laws: federal and state legislation pertaining to employees; regulations concerning wages, hours, working conditions, disability, unemployment compensation, and social security contributions. (See *Department of Labor*.)

law of diminishing returns: term describing the concept that the rate of yield beyond a certain point does not increase in proportion to additional investments.

legal personality: an organization such as a government

or business which can sue or be sued, buy and sell property, and in general assume obligations and liabilities.

letter of credit: See Index.

licenses: state or professional permit to practice a profession or open a business; a means of regulating business, protecting public health, safety, zoning, and in some cases, public morality.

limited partnership: partnership formed by two or more individuals in which at least one partner is fully liable for all the debts of the business, but other partners known as the limited partners have a liability only to the extent of their investment.

Mary Smith wanted to open a restaurant but she did not have enough capital. She offered a limited partnership to her brother and two friends of 10 percent of the total value of the business for each limited partner at a cost of $10,000 each. Mary would run the restaurant and make all the decisions. Each partner would receive 10 percent of the restaurant's profit as long as he kept his money invested in the business. If Mary went broke, each partner would be liable for not more than his investment. Each partner could also sell his partnership to a fellow partner or to an outsider depending on how the partnership agreement was drawn up.

loss leaders: in retailing, special inexpensively priced merchandise offered to complement higher-priced lines and to build store traffic.

management consultant: independent contractor who advises management on the most effective way of achieving its goal.

management controls: a term used to denote the capacity to be in touch with each unit in a business and to be able to respond to changes, adjustments, and needs.

managerial skills: the capacity to cope with responsibility and guide others to carry out the work; may include technical skills, human skills, and conceptual skills.

market research: a survey to project an estimated demand for a product, evaluate type and quality of competition and how affordable the product is to the general populace on a national, state, and local basis; the research should indicate the product's success probability.

marketer's aids: helpful data published by the Small Business Administration and available to the public.

markup: the difference between cost of an item and its selling price.

markup percentage: the markup price expressed in percentages; calculations include cost of the item, the cost of selling the item, and allowance for desired profit.

mean: the sum of a group of numbers divided by the number of individual numbers used.

median: the midpoint of numbers arranged from lowest to highest.

merchandising: those business functions dealing with presenting and selling goods and ideas; includes advertising, display, promotion and direct selling.

merger: the combination of two companies either by the acquisition or assets or the formation of a new company where an exchange of stock would take place.

mode: the number that occurs most frequently in a series of data.

motivation: the reason a worker wants to carry out his or her job.

national brands: brands owned by national manufacturers. (See *brand*.)

National Small Business Association: organization "to foster the birth and vigorous development of independent small business"; concerned with education, foreign trade, labor and taxes; publishes a monthly magazine, *Voice of Small Business*. (See *BEAM*.) The address is:

1604 K Street N.W.
Washington, DC 20006

Occupational Safety and Health Act: a federal law with approximately 22,000 regulations designed to protect employees from work-related accidents, poor illumination, unmarked fire exits, inadequate washrooms and other hazards and sanitation infractions; businesses are required to display at the place of work occupational administration posters.

oligopoly: the domination of an industry by a few large companies.

operating budget: current income and expenditures; does not include capital items.

operating level: the amount of inventory required to maintain normal operations.

organizational chart: the chain of command and reporting structure in a company.

packaging: 1) merchandise—such as soap powder, perishible foods, etc.—that because of its nature needs to be put in a carton or other container; 2) the means used to present a product in the most attractive, salable way.

parity business: a business in which products and services are very much alike.

patent: the right of exclusive proprietorship of an invention granted by the government for a specific period of time.

patent office: part of U.S. Department of Commerce that administers federal trademark laws and all matters pertaining to the granting of patents.

penetration pricing: practice of selling a new product at a low price to induce a large volume of sales; the profit comes from the volume, and the low price discourages fellow manufacturers who have not yet produced the product to compete.

personnel turnover: a term used in personnel referring to how often employees in a company have to be replaced because they are unhappy or because the employees were poorly chosen to begin with.

positioning: stressing unique selling points, emphasizing specific market segments, setting targets; appealing to an identifiable market such as teenagers or senior citizens.

price leader: the one who sets the price; competitors follow suit.

price-lining: offering merchandise at a limited number of set prices in order to simplify the selling job and make choice easier for the consumer. For example, a store may offer two prices for hosiery, a 99¢ line and a $1.99 line.

pricing: establishing a price for goods or services. There are three methods: with the market, below the market, and above the market. A general rule is that a small sales volume requires a relatively high markup, and a large sales volume can bear a reduced markup.

primary-demand advertising: an attempt to increase demand for a type of product—such as cheese, all-cotton clothes, etc.—rather than for a brand; usually sponsored by trade associations.

private brands: brands owned by middlemen such as retailers. (See *brand*.)

Producer Price Index: guideline reflecting the rise or fall of prices for finished goods; includes costs of raw material and general manufacturing costs.

production planning: preparation for the best use of machines, raw materials, and employees.

promoter: 1) one who shows a business, usually a new one, to advantage; 2) a group or organization that plans, creates, and organizes ideas, companies and corporations.

proprietor: 1) person who forms and operates a business; the simplest form of ownership in which business income is taxed as personal income and the owner is personally liable for all claims against the business; 2) legal title to anything such as an automobile, home, or a patent or design.

psychological pricing: method of pricing based on a common belief that an uneven price such as $3.98 appears less expensive to the customer than a rounded number such as $4.00; some retailers choose an uneven number because it forces the clerk to give change and lessens the possibility of a clerk pocketing the even amount of dollars.

public relations: the effort toward developing a favorable public image of a business by projecting positive publicity or doing good works such as donating free merchandise to a fund raiser; making known the company's good works, for example, "we work to keep our community clean."

purchasing: the process of obtaining material for a company.

qualified products list: prepared by various government agencies for their purchasing requirements, a list containing the products and manufacturers that have met essential government specifications. (See *Commerce Business Daily*.)

quota: limit on the amount of a particular item that can legally be imported.

SCORE (Service Corps of Retired Executives) and **ACE (Active Corps of Executives):** experienced men and women who volunteer their time to assist free of charge those who want their business problems analyzed and dealt with, and who in general need an experienced daily hand.

secondary data: statistics gathered not necessarily with a specific business in mind but generally helpful nevertheless.

silent partner: a general partner who is inactive and anonymous except to the active partner(s); depending on the contract carries unlimited liabilities for the obligations of the business.

skimming: a method of pricing whereby a manufacturer charges a higher price for a new product because it is novel and later, when competition enters the market, reduces the price.

Small Business Administration: agency created by the federal government to offer financial assistance, procurement assistance, advocacy of small business and management assistance; has more than 100 offices throughout the nation with special programs to help minorities, veterans, and the socially and economically disadvantaged; puts out valuable publications on small-business' insurance needs, risks, taxes, etc. (See *call*.) The address is:

1441 L Street NW
Washington DC 20416

Small Business Institute: those universities and colleges that enter into formal contracts with the Small Business Administration to provide faculty-supervised management counseling to participating small businesses.

standardization: term to describe the manufacture of identical or uniform goods.

survey: questions asked by phone, mail, or in public to find out product preferences, needs and whatever else will help a business.

syndicate: a group of individuals and/or investment firms, banks and stockbrokers who are temporarily associated together under one manager for some specific business venture, for example, to underwrite a particular security or to invest in a large real estate undertaking such as a shopping center or office complex.

systems analyst: an expert who interprets the company's

needs for information, and devises a computer program that will process the data.

table: a means of presenting data.

tariff: tax on imported goods.

trademark: a brand given legal protection so that the owner has exclusive right to its use. (See *brand*.)

traffic flow: data on foot and vehicular traffic that can advance or impede a business. For instance, a retail store will want to be where there is much foot traffic; a manufacturing concern will want to be near public transportation so that its workers can get to work.

trust: any business or company owning a combination of businesses for the purpose of greater profit or eliminating competition. Antitrust laws restrict the operations of business trusts.

truth in advertising: provision of laws that control advertising and prohibit misleading statements; most of the laws are in the hands of the Federal Trade Commission.

uniform delivery pricing: same delivery price regardless of transportation costs and distance. (See *zone pricing*.)

variables: a term used by statisticians to denote changeable factors.

withholding tax: social security and other federal and state taxes the employer must withhold from the employee's wages. The Internal Revenue Service and state tax agency can supply all the information needed.

zone pricing: arrangement by which customers pay for delivery according to the distance from the manufacturer to the point of delivery. (See *uniform delivery pricing*.)

FOR FURTHER READING

Bonds

Brindze, Ruth. *Investing Money: The Facts About Stocks and Bonds*. Harcourt, Brace and World, 1968.

Darst, David M. *The Complete Bond Book*. McGraw-Hill.

Davis, Lewis. *Dictionary of Banking and Finance*. Totowa, New Jersey: Rowman & Littlefield, 1978.

Understanding Bonds and Preferred Stocks. The New York Stock Exchange, Inc., 1978.

Stock Market Trading Terms

Barnes, Lee, Ph.D., and Feldman, Stephen, Ph.D., *Handbook of Wealth Management*. New York: McGraw-Hill Book Company, 1977

Barnoff, Paul. *Wall Street Thesaurus*. Ivan Obolensky, 1963.

Eiteman, W. J., et al. *Stock Market*. 4th edition. McGraw-Hill, 1966.

Elliott, Ralph N. *An Elementary Introduction Into the Elliott's Wave Theory*. Institute of Economic Finance, 1981.

Flavian, C. *The College Student Introduction to the World of Wall Street*. American Classical College Press, 1974.

Goldberg, I. A., and Gordon, R. A. *How to Read Newspaper Stock Transactions*. Gordon, 1969.

Haft, Richard H. *Investing in Securities*. Englewood Cliffs, New Jersey: Prentice-Hall, Inc., 1975.

Hagin, Robert. *The Dow Jones-Irwin Guide to Modern Portfolio Theory*. Homewood, Illinois: Dow Jones-Irwin, 1979.

Language of Investing Glossary, The. The New York Stock Exchange, Inc., 1978.

Miller, Eugene. *Your Future in Securities*. Rosen Press, 1974.

Mitchell, Lloyd. *How to Make Money in Wall Street Through the Intelligent Use of Price Earning Ratios*. Institute of Economic Finance, 1981.

Standard & Poor's Ratings Guide. McGraw-Hill.

Stock Market & Wall Street: The Essential Knowledge Which Everybody But Absolutely Everybody Ought to Have Of the Stock Market and Wall Street. American Classical College Press (The Essential Knowledge Series Book), 1978.

Understanding Convertible Securities. The New York Stock Exchange, Inc., 1978.

Understanding the New York Stock Exchange. The New York Stock Exchange, Inc., 1976.

Weissman, Rudolph L. *The New Wall Street Facsimile*. Arno, 1975.

Commodities

Kroll, Stanley, and Shishko, Irwin. *The Commodity Futures Market Guide*. New York: Harper & Row, 1973.

Stevenson, Richard A. and Jennings, Edward H. *Fundamentals of Investments*. 2nd edition. St. Paul, Minnesota: West Publishing Co., 1981.

Teweles, Richard J., Ph.D.; Hurlow, Charles V., D.B.A.; and Stone, Herbert L., D.B.A. *The Commodity Futures Trading Guide*. New York: McGraw-Hill Book Co., 1969.

Wuliger, Betty S. *Dollar & Sense*. New York: Random House, 1976.

Money Instruments

Donoghue, William E., and Tilling, Thomas. *William E. Donoghue's Complete Money Market Guide*. New York: Harper & Row, 1980.

Greenwald, Douglas, and Associates. *The McGraw-Hill Dictionary of Modern Economics: A Handbook of Terms and Organizations*. New York: McGraw-Hill Book Co., 1973.

Stigum, Marcia. *The Money Market: Myth, Reality and Practice*. Homewood, Illinois 60430: Dow Jones-Irwin, 1978.

Diamonds and Precious Metals

A Gold Pricing Model. International Gold Corporation Limited, 6455 Fifth Avenue, New York, N.Y. 10022

Beckner, Steven K. *The Hard Money Book*. New York: The Capitalist Reporter Press, 1979.

Carabini, Louis E., ed. *Everything You Need to Know Now About Gold and Silver*. New Rochelle, New York: Arlington House, 1974.

Gold Investment Handbook Statistical Update. International Gold Corporation Limited, 6455 Fifth Avenue, New York, N.Y. 10022

Green, Timothy. *How to Buy Gold*. New York: Walker & Co., 1975.

Persons, Robert H. *The Investor's Encyclopedia of Gold, Silver and Other Precious Metals*. New York: Random House, Inc., and MTS Publishing Corp., 1974.

Rogers, R. *Dictionary of Gems*. Birmingham: Jones & Palmer, Limited. 99 + 100 Albion Street, 1933.

Shipley, Robert Morrill. *Dictionary of Gems and Gemology*. Los Angeles, California: Gemological Institute of America, 541 South Alexandria, 1951.

Szuprowicz, Bohdan O. *How to Invest in Strategic Metals*. New York: St. Martin's Press, 175 Fifth Avenue, 1982.

Turner, W. W. *Gold Coins for Financial Survival.* Nashville, Tennessee: Hermitage Press, 1971.

Vilar, Pierre. *A History of Gold & Money*. London: NLB, 7 Carlisle St., W. 1, 1969.

Real Estate

Allen, Robert D., and Wolfe, Thomas E. *Real Estate Almanac.*™ New York: John Wiley & Sons, 1980.

Arnold Encyclopedia of Real Estate, The. Boston, Massachusetts: Warren, Gorham & Lamont, Inc., 1978.

Estes, Jack. *Real Estate License Preparation Course for The Uniform Examination.* New York: McGraw-Hill, Inc., 1976.

Gross, Jerome S. *Illustrated Encyclopedic Dictionary of Real Estate Terms.* Englewood Cliffs, New Jersey: Prentice-Hall, Inc., 1969.

Language of Real Estate, The. Chicago, Illinois: Real Estate Education Co., 1977.

Nessen, Robert L. *The Real Estate Book*. Boston: Little, Brown and Co., 1981.

Seldin, Maury, ed. *The Real Estate Handbook*. Homewood, Illinois: Dow Jones-Irwin, 1980.

Temple, Douglas M. *Making Money in Real Estate.* Chicago, Illinois: Henry Regnery Co.

Loans and Mortgages

Bryant, Willis R. *Mortgage Lending*. New York: McGraw-Hill Book Co., Inc., 1962.

Clontz, Ralph C., in collaboration with the editors of the Banking Law Journal. *Truth-In-Lending Manual*, revised edition. Boston, Massachusetts: Hanover Lamont Corporation, 1970.

Consumer Credit Guide. Chicago, Illinois: Commerce Clearing House, 1969.

Gross, Robin, and Cullen, Jean V. *Help: The Basics of Borrowing Money*. New York: Times Books, 1980.

Hayes, Rick Stephan. *Business Loans: A Guide to Money Sources and How to Approach Them Successfully*, 2nd ed. Boston, Massachusetts: CBI, d 1980.

How Much Do I Owe? How Much Can I Borrow?: A personal analysis and guide. New York: Dreyfus Publication, Ltd., 1972.

Heckley, Howard H. *Lending Functions of The Federal Reserve Banks: A History*. Washington Publications Services Division of Administrative Services. Board of Governors of the Federal Reserve System, 1973.

Income Opportunities. New York: Arco Publishing Company, 1964.

Jacoby, Neil Herman, and Saulnier, Raymond J. *Term Lending to Business*. New York: National Bureau of Research, 1942.

Johnson, Robert Willard; Johnson, Robert W.; Jordan, Robert L.; and Warren, William D. *Manual on the Federal Trust-In-Lending Law*. Washington, D.C.: National Foundation for Consumer Credit, 1969.

Mayer, Martin, and the editors of Dreyfus Publications. *Give Yourself Credit: The Art of Borrowing*; illustrated by Roy Doty. Dreyfus Publications, 1972.

Pease, Robert H., editor, and Kerwood, Lewis O., M.B.A., Associate editor. *Mortgage Banking*, 2nd edition. New York: McGraw-Hill Book Co., Inc. 1965.

Stevens, Mark. *Leveraged Finance: How to Raise and Invest Cash*. Englewood Cliffs, New Jersey: Prentice-Hall, 1980.

United States Commission on Federal Paperwork. *Small Business Loans.* For sale by the Superintendent of Documents, U.S. Government Printing Office, 1977.

United States Small Business Administration. *Investor Information Manual*. Washington, D.C., 1980.

Insurance

Green, Thomas E. CPCU, CLU, ed.; Osler, Robert W.; Bickley, John S., Ph.D. *Glossary of Insurance Terms*. Santa Monica, California: The Merritt Company, 1661 Ninth Street, 1980.

Ingrisano, John R., ed. *The Insurance Dictionary*, Life and Health Edition. Indianapolis, Indiana: The Research and Review Service of America, Inc., 1978.

Kein, Marianne T. *Insurance Language.* Philadelphia, Pennsylvania: Running Press, 1949.

McIntyre, William Stokes, CP CU/ARM, ed. *Glossary of Insurance and Risk Management Terms*. Rimco, Inc., 1978.

Financial Statements

Gibson, Charles H., and Boyer, Patricia A. *Financial Statement Analysis*. C.B.I. Publishing Co., Inc., Boston, Massachusetts 02210, 1979.

Hobbs, James B., D.B.A., and Moore, Carl L., M.A.,

C.P.A. *Financial Accounting*. South-Western Publishing Co., 1979.

Kendall, Jeffrey Slates. *Simplifying Accounting Language*. Dubuque, Iowa: Hunt Publishing Co., 1979.

Munn, Glenn G., revised and enlarged by F. L. Garcia. *Encyclopedia of Banking and Finance*. Boston: Bankers Publishing Co., 1973.

Understanding Financial Statements. Published by The New York Stock Exchange, Inc. with data compiled as of March 1981.

Investing In A Small Business

Albert, Kenneth J. *How to Pick the Right Small Business Opportunity*. New York: McGraw-Hill, 1977.

Allen, Louis L. *Starting and Succeeding in Your Own Small Business*. Forward by Frank L. Tucker; Introduction by Wilford L. White. New York: Grosset & Dunlap, 1968.

Bennett, Vivo, and Clagett, Cricket. *1001 Ways to Be Your Own Boss*. Englewood Cliffs, New Jersey: Prentice-Hall, 1976.

Bentley Clark Associates, Office of Policy. *Planning and Budgeting*. Planning and Program Evaluation Division, U.S. Small Business Administration, 1979.

Brannen, William H. *Successful Marketing For Your Small Business*. Englewood Cliffs, New Jersey: Prentice-Hall, 1978.

Bunn, Verne A. *Buying and Selling a Small Business*. Washington, D.C.: Small Business Administration, Superintendent of Documents, U.S. Government Printing Office, 1969.

Bunzel, John E. *The American Small Businessman.* New York: Knopf, 1962.

Cahill, Jane. *Can a Small Store Succeed*? New York: Fairchild Publications, 1966.

Christensen, Carl Roland. *Management Succession in Small and Growing Enterprises.* Boston, Massachusetts: Division of Research, Graduate School of Business Administration, Harvard University, 1953.

Cole, Roland J., and Tegeler, Philip D. *Government Requirements of Small Business.* Lexington, Massachusetts: Lexington Books, 1980.

Dean, Sandra Linville. *How to Advertise: A Handbook for Small Business.* Wilmington, Delaware: Enterprise Publishers, 1980.

Dibble, Donald M., ed. *How to Plan and Finance a Growing Business.* Revised and updated edition. Fairfield, California: Entrepreveur Press, 1980.

Easley, Eddie V.; Lundgren, Earl F.; and Wolk, Harry I. *Contemporary Business: Challenges and Opportunities.* New York: West Publishing Co., 1978.

Fram, Eugene H. W. *What You Should Know About Small Business Marketing.* Dobbs Ferry, New York: Oceana Publishers, 1968.

Frantz, Forrest H. *Successful Small Business Management.* Englewood Cliffs, New Jersey: Prentice-Hall, 1978.

Gross, Eugene L.; Cancel, Adrian R.; and Figueroa, Oscar. *Small Business Works*! Illustrated by Eugene L. Gross. New York: Amacom, 1977.

Hammer, Marian Behan. *The Complete Handbook of How to Start and Run a Moneymaking Business in Your Home.* West Nyack, New York: Parker Publishing Co., 1975.

Key, Denise A., ed. *Encyclopedia of Associations.* Volume I, National Organizations of the U.S., 16th edition, Gale

Research Co., Detroit, Michigan: Book Tower, 1981.

Lane, Marc J. *Legal Handbook for Small Business.* New York: Anacom, 1977.

Lowry, Albert L. *How to Become Financially Successful by Owning Your Own Business.* New York: Simon & Schuster, 1981.

Stanworth, M., and Curnan, V. *Management Motivation in the Smaller Business.* Epping: Gower Press, 1973.

Stevens, Mark. *36 Small Business Mistakes and How to Avoid Them.* West Nyack, New York: Parker, 1978.

Taylor, Frederick John. *How to Be Your Own Boss.* London: Business Books, 1975.

INDEX